Embracing Creation

"The authors combine their expertise in the fields of theology, restoration history, and wildlife biology to provide readers with a fresh and long-overdue look at a biblical theology of creation. As they take us through Scripture, they demonstrate definitively the centrality of that theology and the truth that God is in the process of redeeming all of creation. The authors call us to remember God's story and then to participate with God in restoring not the past but the future redemption of creation. One will leave the reading of this book with a deeper appreciation for the physical world and a renewed commitment to embrace God's forgotten mission."

— **David Bland,** professor of homiletics, director of the Doctor of Ministry program, Harding School of Theology

"Everyone now knows about the deep seriousness of our environmental crisis. These authors make a vigorous, compelling response to that crisis with acute theological probes. They mobilize the entire witness of Scripture and make clear that the well-being of creation is no incidental matter to the gospel. That well-being, as they show, is a primary gift and intent of the creator and a primary human task. The good news pertains to all of creation, so the argument goes, or it is no good news at all."

— **Walter Brueggemann,** Columbia Theological Seminary

EMBRACING
CREATION

EMBRACING CREATION

GOD'S FORGOTTEN MISSION

JOHN MARK HICKS,
BOBBY VALENTINE,
& MARK WILSON

LEAFWOOD
PUBLISHERS
an imprint of Abilene Christian University Press

EMBRACING CREATION
God's Forgotten Mission

LEAFWOOD
P U B L I S H E R S
an imprint of Abilene Christian University Press

Copyright © 2016 by John Mark Hicks, Bobby Valentine, and Mark Wilson

ISBN 979-0-89112-336-1 | LCCN 2015051077

Printed in the United States of America

LIBRARY OF CONGRESS CATALOGING-IN-PUBLICATION DATA
Names: Hicks, John Mark, author.
Title: Embracing creation : God's forgotten mission / by John Mark Hicks,
   Bobby Valentine, and Mark Wilson.
Description: 1st [edition]. | Abilene : Abilene Christian University Press,
   2016.
Identifiers: LCCN 2015051077 | ISBN 9780891123361 (trade paper)
Subjects: LCSH: Creation. | Ecotheology. | Human ecology--Religious
   aspects--Christianity. | Redemption--Christianity.
Classification: LCC BT695 .H53 2016 | DDC 231.7/65--dc23
LC record available at http://lccn.loc.gov/2015051077

Cover design by Greg Jackson
Interior text design by Sandy Armstrong

For information contact:
Abilene Christian University Press
ACU Box 29138
Abilene, Texas 79699

1-877-816-4455
www.acupressbooks.com

16 17 18 19 20 21 / 7 6 5 4 3 2 1

All creatures of our God and King
Lift up your voice and with us sing,
Alleluia! Alleluia!
Thou burning sun with golden beam,
Thou silver moon with softer gleam!

Thou rushing wind that art so strong
Ye clouds that sail in Heaven along,
O praise Him! Alleluia!
Thou rising moon, in praise rejoice,
Ye lights of evening, find a voice!

Thou flowing water, pure and clear,
Make music for thy Lord to hear,
Alleluia! Alleluia!
Thou fire so masterful and bright,
Thou givest man both warmth and light.

Dear mother earth, who day by day
Unfoldest blessings on our way,
O praise Him! Alleluia!
The flowers and fruits that in thee grow,
Let them His glory also show.

Let all things their Creator bless,
And worship Him in humbleness,
O praise Him! Alleluia!
Praise, praise the Father, praise the Son,
And praise the Spirit Three in One!

O praise Him! O praise Him!
Alleluia! Alleluia! Alleluia!

—St. Francis of Assisi (1225)
  Translated by William H. Draper (1919)

Acknowledgments

We are grateful for the opportunity to share this material with readers. All of us have spent a number of years thinking about the place of creation in God's redemptive story.

We thank Jason Fikes for providing his input, editorial work, and encouragement. We appreciate the work he is doing at ACU Press.

We are also grateful for a group of readers who not only read the manuscript before publication but also met with us for a full day of discussion about its strengths and weaknesses. Thank you Jeff Wischkaemper, Andy Walker, Grant Azbell, Van Gilbert, Gipson Baucum, Chris Keaton, Jeff Brown, Tim Parish, Wayne Dunaway, Heath Pickard, and Robbie McKenzie.

We are, of course, most grateful for the support of our families in the preparation of this book. We love you all!

Contents

Introduction

An Invitation to Hear the Story

God's plan is not to abandon this world,
the world which he said was "very good." Rather,
he intends to remake it. And when he does he will
raise all his people to new bodily life to live in it.
That is the promise of the Christian gospel.

—N. T. Wright[1]

The earliest inkling of this book goes back nearly half a century. I (Mark) grew up in the 1960–70s. As a youth with an unusually high interest in both biology and theology, I felt disappointed with the teaching I heard in various church settings, which only superficially addressed God's momentous act of creation. I understood some were reluctant to initiate potentially contentious discussions of complex scientific issues seemingly at odds with Biblical teachings, but I also experienced a deeper unease as well, albeit faint and difficult to express at the time. The teaching I remember did not challenge us with the responsibility to care for creation, which is God's inaugural mandate for humanity (Gen. 1:26–28). God explicitly tasked us with "ruling" over creation, and I heard little attention given to what that meant.

The grandeur of creation innately prompts us to carefully consider whether we have been faithful to our earliest divine commission—to responsibly rule over what God has made. However, churches typically consign creation stewardship far below other topics. How many have heard someone devote an entire sermon or Bible lesson to the proper care for God's creation? Perhaps there are a few.

We invite you to walk with us through God's love story with creation. As we journey together, perhaps the importance of this topic will emerge more clearly—not only from an agricultural or ecological standpoint but also in terms of Christian character and mission in the world.

Many are surprised "Christians" have any interest in properly caring for the resources of the world we inhabit. Whatever the causes of such perceptions, whether real or imagined, the biblical story motivates and equips believers with a love of creation patterned after the Creator's love. That story invites us to embrace the vocation for which God created us and to appreciate the deep love God has for creation.

History reveals cultural, political, and social influences have all too often co-opted or suppressed truth in its various forms (scientific, ethical, etc.), even biblical truth. The first chapter notes some of these influences, which have often hindered our reading of Scripture. A proper understanding of God's care for the entirety of creation, including land and animals, is a fundamental starting point for developing a biblical, holistic Christian outlook befitting our Creator's intent. As best we can, we intend to filter out extraneous influences and carefully examine what Scripture says about the relationships between God, humanity, and creation.

We hope the perspective advanced in this book provides an overarching, comprehensive awareness of our spiritual past, present, and future as we seek to experience richer and more joyous lives here and now. We hope to gain a greater awareness of biblical promises and their fulfillment, increased appreciation for the significance of creation's goodness, a more benevolent and enthusiastic attitude for creation in the present, and an increased anticipation of a joyous future.

To tell God's story, we begin with Israel because that is where God began a history of renewal and redemption. We walk through Israel's story and songs by embracing our primordial vocation in Genesis, participating in Israel's praise, and reveling in Israel's hope. This is God's love story with creation.

Next, keeping our eyes on Jesus, we anchor our theology of creation and new creation in the work of the Messiah who furthers the values of Israel in his ministry and is himself the beginning of new creation. We follow Jesus in his Jubilee ministry, which calls us into new life. We participate in God's love story with creation as we practice conservation within creation and extend the hospitality of Jubilee.

Finally, recognizing that God's promises to Abraham are fulfilled in Jesus the Messiah, the heir of all things, we reflect on the meaning of the incarnation, the beginning of new creation in resurrection, and our inheritance, which is a renewed cosmos where we will reign with God forever. God's love for creation issues in its renewal, and this is the Christian hope.

If this is our inheritance, how then should we live, and how do we think about "restoration" as a restoration movement? The concluding chapter offers a renewed vision for restoration in the light of God's goal for creation.

We hope to foster greater appreciation for the vast goodness of God. The last benevolent act in the formation of the cosmos in Genesis 1 was to invest humanity with godlikeness so we might glorify the Creator through responsible dominion over a creation of unimaginable wonders.

God's love story with creation invites us to participate in God's love for creation—to appreciate God's faithfulness to it, to lead creation in the praise of God, and to rise to the challenge of wise care for the earth and its resources, conforming to our Creator's intent. This is our forgotten mission, assigned by God!

The Bible's open secret, forgotten in modern times, is just how much God loves creation. "To the LORD your God belong the heaven, even the highest heavens, the earth and everything in it" (Deut. 10:14). Creation does not belong to human beings. It belongs to God, and it is the Messiah's inheritance. We are only stewards and junior partners, though we are coheirs with Christ.

May we celebrate creation with God as we come to a better understanding and enthusiastically embrace our divine commission to responsibly care for creation as well as enjoy it.

CHAPTER ONE

What Will Happen to God's Creation?

The Nature of Christian Hope

For dear to God is the earth Christ trod.
No place but is holy ground . . .
This is my Father's world, a wanderer I may roam
Whate'er my lot, it matters not,
My heart is still at home.
—Maltbie D. Babcock, "This is My Father's World" (1901)

When Christ shall come, with shout of acclamation,
And take me home, what joy shall fill my heart.
Then I shall bow, in humble adoration,
And then proclaim: "My God, how great Thou art!"
—Carl Gustaf Boberg, "How Great Thou Art!" (1891)

Where will we spend eternity? What will become of
the earth? The above hymns paint two different pictures, and we
sing both.

Most hymns, for the last two hundred years, sing of a home
for the immortal soul in a celestial city with a "mansion just over

the hilltop."[1] "This world is not my home," goes one of the more popular songs, "I'm just a-passing through."[2] Heaven is home, and "just over in Gloryland, we'll live eternally."[3] Or, the ever popular,

> *When the dead in Christ shall rise,*
> *and the glory of His resurrection share;*
> *when His chosen ones shall gather*
> *to their home beyond the skies,*
> *and the roll is called up yonder,*
> *I'll be there.*[4]

One well-known hymn rejoices in God's "new creation," which is only complete in heaven:

> *Finish then thy new creation,*
> *Pure and spotless let us be.*
> *Let us see thy great salvation*
> *Perfectly restored in thee.*
> *Changed from glory into glory,*
> *Till in heaven we take our place.*[5]

There was a time, however, when hymns envisioned a triumphant reclamation of the earth for God's kingdom. In this vision, God renews the earth, and the kingdom of God fills it: "From out of chaos wild, / New beauty He will bring."[6] Or,

> *Thou hast said, and Thou art true,*
> *That the world Thou shalt renew;*
> *This sweet promise now we plead;*
> *May it be fulfilled with speed.*[7]

These songs are now lost in a distant past. The vision of a renewed earth has practically disappeared from twentieth-century Protestant hymnology, though it is still present in Eastern Orthodox liturgy and other traditions.

Given the popularity of "heaven" as a celestial city in our hymnology, it is little wonder a renewed earth sounds so strange, if not "worldly." As Basil of Caesarea (d. 379) wrote long ago in *On the Faith*, "As we worship, so we believe."

Blurred Vision

Throughout the centuries, Christianity has envisioned "heaven" (the eternal state) in two different ways. One is the spiritual vision model, which identifies the present heavenly dwelling place of God as our eternal home. The other is the new creation model, which emphasizes a material earth (renewed, transfigured, or recreated from its ashes) where the resurrected redeemed live with God forever.[8]

Today, "heaven" falls into these two broad conceptualizations. One is spiritual (immaterial) because fire will annihilate the present cosmos. The other is material (physical) because a new creation will emerge from this old one. The former emphasizes a mystical, beatific vision of God as the essence of heaven, while the latter stresses how God dwells on a renewed earth with redeemed humanity. The former identifies "spirit" as the reality to which humans aspire, while the latter affirms the material integrity of the new creation in the eternal state.

Many Christians are surprised that some have ever believed in a future renewed earth because surely the earth, with all its sorrows and woes, is something we want to escape. So what happened?

Ancient Roots

Historically, two ideological trends have deeply shaped Christian thinking about the earth and the eternal state. One is a philosophic tradition known as Platonism, and the other is a Christian heresy called Gnosticism.

Though Platonism appears in several forms, it usually denigrates the body and affirms an immortal soul. The goal of life is to return to God, free of the body and earth's materiality. Neo-Platonism pictured true believers ascending through the "seven spheres of heaven" as the "soul travels" to God where, with "other spirits," they "spend eternity 'singing with sweet voice to God.'"[9] Heaven is the mystical communion of saints with God as disembodied spirits.

Gnosticism was Christian Platonism on steroids. A diverse system rooted in dualism, Gnosticism suggested creation (materiality) is the work of evil powers while the spiritual (immaterial) is a higher order. Put simply, materiality is negative (evil) but spirituality is positive (good). Consequently, Gnostics denied (1) the Father created the world, (2) the Son really became flesh, (3) the sacraments are true means of grace by the Spirit, and (4) the resurrection of the body. Their vision of "heaven" was wholly spiritual, and the resurrection of Jesus transformed him into "an imperishable aeon," which gives "us the way to immortality."[10]

The early church, however, strongly affirmed the goodness of creation (materiality). Therefore, creation, incarnation, and resurrection were deeply entrenched in its worship and life, and it denied a Neo-Platonic or Gnostic "heaven."

Irenaeus (d. 202), Bishop of Lyons, defended Christianity against Gnosticism. Central to his understanding was (1) the goodness of creation by the will of the Father and (2) the authentic humanity of the incarnated Son. The Father of Jesus graciously created the world from nothing.[11] Consequently, participation in creation is not inconsistent with God's own goodness. Jesus was "truly" human and "truly God."[12] The incarnation affirmed the goodness of creation, since God cannot participate in moral inferiority, much less something evil.

Irenaeus notes that Jesus, as God incarnate, replayed every aspect of human existence in order to renew human life.[13] This redeemed humanity from birth to death, including the spirit, soul, and body. In his resurrection, Jesus redeemed not only the body but creation as a whole because his body was part of creation. For though "the fashion of the world passes away," Irenaeus writes, neither the "substance" nor "essence of the creation" is "annihilated."[14] When humanity arises from the dead in their immortal bodies, creation will rise anew, freed from its bondage to corruption (Rom. 8:19–23). Humanity then receives the "promise of the inheritance of the earth."[15]

Modern Context

While the roots of the denigration or neglect of creation are ancient, modernity has deeply shaped the attitudes of believers toward creation. Indeed, modern ideological, cultural, and pragmatic agendas practically preclude any thorough revisiting of biblical texts about creation. This baggage so colors our reading that we are perfectly satisfied with a mansion above rather than a renewed creation.

Human Autonomy. God shared with humanity the divine mission to care for the Garden of Eden—to protect it and expand it. Humanity, deceived by the serpent, pursued independence, which in effect was a rejection of their creaturehood. They wanted to be "like God."

We embrace this trajectory when we assert dominion over creation and fail to mirror God's interests, values, and goals. We use creation as we desire rather than in conformity with God's mission. We presume creation is ours to do with as we please. We generate our own goal for creation and we lie at the center of it. In essence, we become the measure of what is right and good as we live within God's creation. We forget—even reject—how God created the world for God rather than for us and how it belongs to God (Ps. 24:1; Lev. 25:23).

Modern Utilitarianism. We tend to judge the worth of something only insofar as it is pleasing, useful, or profitable *for us*. This assumes creation is about us, for us, and centered on us. We can, so the argument might run, use creation in whatever way it benefits us. The primary criterion for the use of creation, then, becomes utility rather than God's mission.

The potential adverse implications of this utilitarian outlook are largely based in ignorance and arrogance. If we are ignorant of the true value of assets that belong to someone else, is it proper to assign overall value to them based only on their aesthetic appeal or usefulness to us personally? For example, if one walks into a private art gallery and deems only some of the art on display aesthetically appealing, does that devalue the rest of the exhibits? In other words, we cannot determine the value of creation simply by assessing how it benefits us. There are larger factors at work—most importantly God's own goal for creation and its role in the divine mission.

Learning more about creation often increases the value of various facets as we come to a greater appreciation of their interconnected purposes. Bees illustrate this. Most of us do not concern ourselves with these insects—which buzz around our flower gardens and the dandelions—until they get into our car while we are driving! Given the overwhelming problems already in our world (terrorism, homelessness, unemployment), it almost seems laughable that scientists concern themselves with the mysterious, large-scale disappearance of bees in the United States. But when we learn an estimated 30 percent of all food (nuts, vegetables, and fruits) consumed in North America result from plants directly pollinated by bees, the value of these insects suddenly upsurges. Human arrogance and autonomy assign value to some aspects of creation based on their perceived utility and deny similar valuations to other aspects of God's creation we do not yet understand.

Social Darwinism. This is the survival of the fittest, which is not just about biological evolution. Rather, this ideology infects modern politics and economics as well as environmental ethics. In effect, it drives empire-building as well as the exploitation of natural resources for economic wealth.

When racial groups, animals, and natural resources are only an arena in which the "biggest and baddest" conquer, Social Darwinism reigns. Many economic policies, especially in relation to the environment, are Darwinian in nature. Often, greed—as an expression of this ideology—seeks to master creation rather than conserve and safeguard it. Rather than loving creation, a "survival of the fittest" mentality results in the manipulation of creation for human self-interest, which is generally politically or economically motivated. Modern humanity, particularly empires and industry, tends to use creation rather than enjoy it, abuse it rather than conserve it.

Shirked Responsibility. Unfortunately, we tend to shirk personal responsibility for creation care because we believe other people or another entity (usually the government) should bear the responsibility for maintaining a healthy environment. Part of this stems from the magnitude of the problem at hand. Obviously, none of us can single-handedly clean up a Superfund site, restore huge swaths of rainforest cleared for agricultural production, or restore salmon runs to rivers blocked by dams. In view of the scale of the problem, our best personal efforts at caring for, restoring, and protecting God's wonderful creation seem insignificant even if they are fully successful.

In the beginning, God blessed humanity, and in that blessing, called humanity to take responsibility for creation (Gen. 1:26–28). This blessing will continue as long as we pursue the vocation God gave us. The Great Commission (Matt. 28:18–20) is another divine mandate to humans of similar scale and import of the Genesis 1:26–28 directives. However, we would never even consider hoping other people or "the government" would undertake that lofty task on our behalf merely because, at first glance, the scale of the undertaking makes it seemingly impossible. We know that individual Christians everywhere need to combine their efforts and work together to achieve the lofty goal of making disciples throughout the world. Because the task is important to Jesus, we assume he will work alongside us (Matt. 28:20) and bless our efforts. Similarly, when we personally engage in various aspects of creation care with the gifts, talents, and opportunities bestowed to each of us, we should also fully expect the blessing promised to those who engage in proper creation care activity: "That it may go well with you and you may live long" (Deut. 22:7).

Modern Religious Movements. Strong pietistic and revivalist streams in the eighteenth and nineteenth centuries, emphasizing individual salvation and heavenly rewards, promoted the spiritualized understanding of heaven, and it became the most popular vision in the late nineteenth and early twentieth centuries, especially during the Great Depression. Many of our "heaven" songs arose in the context of the Great Depression, which is understandable, since many wanted to escape the woes and tragedies of that era. Those songs brought tremendous comfort. The Depression era, along with an individualistic understanding of salvation ("I was saved") and a revivalism that promised individual rewards in heaven, shaped our picture of heaven from the 1920s forward.

At the same time, some dispensational premillennialists—a new theological movement in the late nineteenth century—gave vivid expression to this, especially the *Scofield Bible*, first published in 1909. Later popularizations of dispensational premillennial thought have suggested that after the thousand-year reign of Christ on earth, the saints "fly away" to heaven, which is their permanent spiritual abode, and then "God will incinerate the universe, probably in an atomic reaction that disintegrates all matter as we know it."[16]

This individualism and yearning for rewards in an escapist reality was emphasized by the growth of a prosperity gospel. Over the years, this message has been heralded in some of the largest churches in the world. This gospel has many names, such as the "name it and claim it" gospel, the "blab it and grab it" gospel, the "health and wealth" gospel, the "word of faith" movement, the "gospel of success," and the "positive confession" theology. This craving for individual blessing and reward adapts God's gospel to the categories of modern consumerist-capitalist categories.

This prosperity gospel locates the purpose of faith in the acquisition of wealth and status so as to be "at ease in Zion" (Amos 6:1). Materialism, or the accumulation of stuff, by its very nature interprets the world through utilitarian and consumerist lenses. If this drives our spiritual life, then creation has no real value because it might stand in the way of such acquisitions, and it certainly does not matter in terms of our heavenly rewards. In contrast, the God-affirmed goodness of creation—its beauty and priceless value as

God's own handiwork—is at considerable odds with the prevalent prosperity gospels paraded about in the United States.

Why Is This Important?

Why should we care what happens to God's good earth?

At one level, some don't show much concern because their primary interest is utilitarian—that is, the earth needs to survive until everyone flies away to heaven. In that situation, the earth is treated as garbage to be burned. At another level, some don't care about the earth's future because the main point of "heaven" is living with God rather than *where* we live with God. Consequently, it is thought, we should shelve this conversation because it has no real relevance to God's ultimate goal, which is to live with us in glory. As such, this question is often regarded as not only secondary but also harmful because it places an emphasis upon creation that is seemingly incongruent with what we suppose is God's ultimate concern.

We believe this misses a central theme in biblical theology, and the loss of this theme hinders our understanding of God's story. It misses God's interest in land, inheritance, and a dwelling place with and for the people of God.

Loving creation and recognizing its major role in God's story is important because creation matters to God. God created something "very good," and any theology that ultimately annihilates this good does not take seriously how much God rejoices and delights in creation. We love creation because God loves it, and God created what God wanted. God created a cosmic temple in which to dwell, and God intends to glorify this temple. Creation—from its beginning, to creation care in Israel, to Jesus's Jubilee ministry, to the new heaven and new earth—is integral to the story of God and humanity from beginning to eternity.

It is also important because the nature of salvation is at stake. As we will see in the coming sections, salvation is not only personal and communal but also cosmic. Redemption is not directed solely at the human "spirit" or "immortal soul" (the Bible never says our souls are immortal). On the contrary, redemption includes our bodies, and our bodies are part of God's good creation. The redemption of our bodies is also the redemption of creation. The resurrection of our bodies is the Christian hope and at the heart of the nature of salvation itself. God intends to save what God created and redeem it from the curse.

Further, this is important because our human identity is tied to creation. We were created to share dominion over creation; we were created as images in God's cosmic temple. We cannot be human without creation, since our human identity is directly linked with the human vocation to serve and protect creation as God's royal priests. To be human is to be a creature, and to be a creature is live within a creation. Humanity and creation are bound together before God, and to separate one from the other is to leave both incomplete.

Lastly, it is important because Jesus is the firstborn of new creation. When the Son became flesh, the Word joined himself to creation and united God with creation. The incarnation means God secured the eternal existence of creation because the Son is forever human and thus forever shares our creaturehood as our elder brother. Moreover, the Son transformed human existence—and thus creation's as well—through death when he was raised as the firstborn from the dead. His resurrection is the beginning of new creation, and the body of Jesus is part of the new creation just as our own resurrected bodies will participate in new creation. Creation is important because it will be made new in the resurrection, which includes not only our bodies but the dwelling place of God as well, the new heaven and new earth.

CONCLUSION

The new creation model is a historic position within the church, but modern developments as well as ancient heresies have blurred our vision. In this book, we intend to tell the story of God's love for creation, God's invitation for us to participate in that love story, and God's redemption of creation through Jesus the Messiah.

BULLET POINTS

- The present earth will be renewed or transfigured, the resurrected saints will live upon it, and God will descend to dwell with humanity.
- The new creation model is an ancient understanding rather than a recent innovation by fringe groups.
- Recent historical developments have blinded biblical readers to the biblical emphasis on creation care.

QUESTIONS

1. Which of the two models, the spiritual or new creation vision of the eternal state, is most prominent in your context? Have you had much exposure to the other?

2. In what ways have modern movements shaped our understanding—as well as appreciation or depreciation—of creation as part of God's story?

3. Why are material resurrection and a renewed earth so
   important in a new creation model? What is at stake in
   such a discussion?

Part I

The Biblical Narrative

CHAPTER TWO

A Cathedral of Praise

God, Creation, and Human Vocation

Thus says the Lord:
The heavens are my throne,
and the earth is my footstool;
where is the house you will build for me,
and where is my resting place?
My hand made all these things,
and all these things belong to me, declares the Lord.

—Isa. 66:1–2a; our translation

One of the most corrosive dangers humanity faces
is arrogance. How people relate to the natural world is a case in
point. Historically, and even now, we tend to act as if we are the
center of the cosmos, and we will use it as we please. Nature, in
effect, is for us and about us.

Isaiah 66 sees it differently. After envisioning the creation of a
new heaven and new earth in Isaiah 65:17–25, Yahweh announces
a few fundamental truths about creation: it *belongs to God*, it is
God's house, and it is where *God lives*.

Isaiah's words reach forward to the renewal of God's house in the new heaven and new earth when "all flesh shall come to worship" Yahweh (66:22–23), and they also remind Israel how their present temple is too small for Yahweh since God's presence fills the heavens and the earth. They also echo God's original intent—to dwell with humanity in restful Sabbath within God's good creation.

Creation as God's House

The earth was a chaotic void,
and darkness covered the face of the deep,
while the Spirit of God hovered over the face the waters.

Then God saw everything made and, Wow!, it was really good.

Then, when God had completed the accomplished work, God rested on the seventh day from the accomplished work. Consequently, God blessed the seventh day and sanctified it because on it God rested from the work accomplished in making [the heavens and the earth].

—Gen. 1:2, 31a; 2:2–3; our translation

God did not create the cosmos in order to annihilate it but to dwell within it. Creation is a divine temple in which God lives even though it cannot contain God's fullness.

In some ancient creation myths, the gods built their own heavenly sanctuaries when they finished their creative work (or battles) and sat down on their heavenly thrones to rule their subjects. Yahweh is different. Yahweh constructs a heavenly temple not out of brick and mortar but out of earth and sky. Architectural imagery is a common metaphor for creation in the Hebrew Bible. For example, when Yahweh interrogated Job, the initial questions are framed in architectural images:

Where were you when I laid the earth's foundations?

Who determined its measurements—surely you know!

Or who stretched the line upon it?

On what were its bases sunk,

or who laid its cornerstone?

Or who shut in the sea with doors

and prescribed bounds for it,

set bars and doors. (Job 38:4–10; our translation)

In other words, God erected a building, a house, a temple—creation is a cathedral of praise.

Another reflection of ancient Near Eastern culture is the language of building and filling. Ancient kings and mythological gods built houses and then provisioned them by filling them. This is the pattern of Genesis 1:1–31. God creates space and then fills it, which is the essence of wisdom in creation theology (compare Prov. 3:19–20 with Prov. 24:3–4).

Table 2.1

Days	Created habitable space	Days	Filled the space for life
First	Light	Fourth	Sun, moon, and stars
Second	Sky	Fifth	Birds and fish
Third	Land, sea, and vegetation	Sixth	Animals and humanity

The psalmist parallels the creation of the earth with the construction of the tabernacle: "He built his sanctuary like the heights, like the earth that he established forever" (Ps. 78:69). The tabernacle, though a poor representative of the earth, was the initial step toward the renewal of God's redemptive presence. God's glory filled the tabernacle (Ex. 40) and then later the temple (2 Chron. 6:40–7:3). When humanity was excluded from Eden, God's sanctuary, God did not give up but pursued humanity through the calling of

Abraham, dwelling in Israel's tabernacle and then the temple. In time, God "tabernacled" in the flesh as Israel's Messiah (John 1:14).

When God finished the temple of creation, God "rested" in it. God came to dwell in it, love humanity, walk with them in the Garden, and enjoy the *shalom* of Eden as a divine sanctuary. The Garden of Eden was not an agricultural field but something analogous to one of the seven wonders of the ancient world, the Hanging Gardens of Babylon. The Garden of Eden was the place of repose, joy, and delight for God's icons (images) much like ancient royalty would include gardens within their palace structures. The heavens and the earth, as Isaiah wrote, are God's resting place, just as the temple was God's resting place in Israel (2 Chron. 6:41; Ps. 132:8). God's temple is the heavens and the earth, and the whole creation is God's home. The Garden of Eden, the divine sanctuary of God's cosmic temple, is where God rested with humanity in delightful fellowship (Gen. 2:2–3, 15).

Human Vocation in God's House

> *God blessed them, and God said to them, "Be fruitful and multiply, and fill the earth and subdue it; and have dominion over the fish of the sea and over the birds of the air and over every living thing that moves upon the earth."*
> —Genesis 1:28

> *The Lord God took the* adam *and rested (placed)* adam *in the Garden of Eden to serve and protect it.*
> —Genesis 2:15; our translation

God placed living, breathing "images" within the divine sanctuary. As the image of God, human beings represent God within the cosmos, and God shares with humanity the divine tasks of governing, caring for, and loving creation.

These identify humanity's vocation and invite humanity into God's missional goal for creation. God invites humanity to flourish, fill the whole earth, subdue the cosmos, and protect the divine sanctuary. God intends for Eden to expand and fill the earth as humanity faithfully participates in God's mission. We are God's junior partners in that mission.

Multiply and Fill
This is humanity's expansionistic function.

God "rested" humanity in the Garden. The Hebrew Bible uses this word to describe divine and human rest on the seventh day (Ex. 20:11; 23:12; cf. Deut. 5:14), God's gift of rest to Israel in the land (Deut. 25:19; Josh. 1:13, 15; 1 Chron. 23:25; 2 Chron. 14:6), and God's habitation of the temple (2 Chron. 6:41). God created *adam* (the human being) from the ground (*adamah*) and placed him in the Garden to rest with God as a royal priest in Eden.

Eden, however, was not a static reality. God intended humanity to multiply and fill the whole earth. God intended to expand Eden until it filled the earth, until everything was "Holy to the Lord" (Zech. 14:20). Humanity, as well as animal life, was to populate the earth, and God "formed" the earth "to be inhabited" (Isa. 45:18). God multiplied and filled the earth with glory through the praise of God's creatures (cf. Gen. 1:22; 8:17; 9:1, 7). God multiplied Israel (Gen. 47:27; Ex. 1:7; Lev. 26:9; Jer. 3:16), and later multiplied the church (Acts 6:1, 7; 9:31; 12:24) as an embodiment of this original vision.

Nevertheless, when humanity failed to cooperate, God scattered them. Yahweh scattered humanity at Babel, Israel through exile, and the church through persecution. The divine mission was to fill everything—the heavens and the earth—and everyone with God's glory (Gen. 1:28; 9:1; Isa. 27:6; Ps. 72:19).

Subdue

This is humanity's creative function.

As Creator, God brought order out of chaos. Hovering over the waters enclosed in darkness, God brought order to an uninhabitable earth, a chaotic void. God subdued the earth to provide habitable space, and then God filled the space with life.

Unfortunately, some believe the call to "subdue" empowers humanity to exploit the earth and deplete its resources. On the contrary, "subdue" partners with God's creative work to bring order out of chaos.

The seven days of creation did not rid the cosmos of chaos. Darkness still exists, the waters still exist, and a chaos figure—the serpent—entered Eden itself. God called the light good but not the darkness. God did not remove the waters but bounded them. Outside of Eden, chaos exists within creation.

Humanity partners with God to subdue the remaining chaos. This ordering includes things as diverse as domesticating a field for crops or goats for milk as well as developing software programs to bring order to a chaotic mass of data.

To subdue the earth means to partner in God's creative work; it does not mean abusing or exploiting creation. Whatever chaos remains in creation, humanity is called to subdue it and order it for life in partnership with God.

Rule

This is humanity's royal vocation.

Too often we hear "dominion" in tyrannical, oppressive, militaristic, or manipulative ways, but this is not how God rules. As images of God, we rule in the likeness of God.

For example, the kings of Israel, though they did not always effectively do so, represented God in the nation. God intended them to rule with justice and mercy. Psalm 72 reminds Israel what *dominion* means—the humble exercise of power in the service of mercy (cf. Lev. 25:43, 46, 53). Their rule was supposed to be more like how a shepherd "rules" (cf. Ezek. 34:4) rather than how a dictator "rules." Far from exploitation and abuse, God's imagers rule as servants who give life. They benevolently care for creation.

This gains greater clarity when we recognize we are corulers with God. God *shares* dominion with us. We are coworkers, junior partners. This is our identity, and it is part of our mission to develop the full potential of creation as we lovingly care for it and gratefully enjoy it. We pursue familial, social, and communal *shalom* as we embody the justice and mercy of God within creation.

This vocation involves every aspect of human life. The arts (music, literature, fine art) are expressions of human creativity. Technology manages resources, medicine serves wholeness, and social structures shape community. These are part of the human vocation—our partnership with God—as corulers and cocreators within creation.

This means that no work is "secular," as if it is disconnected from our missional identity. Every good work—no matter how "secular"—participates in the mission of God.

As participants in community, human beings are called into multiple kinds of jobs or different vocational careers. We choose these careers as means to love God and serve our neighbors. Through these careers, we participate in the mission of God.

Medical professionals partner with God in healing. Financial counselors partner with God as they mediate justice for creditors and mercy for debtors. Professionals in the legal community partner with God as they pursue justice. Environmental biologists partner with God as they preserve and care for creation.

Partnering with God toward the fulfillment of the mission of God is ministry in the kingdom of God. Nurses, counselors, biologists, and lawyers corule with God. Through their careers, they are ministers and royal priests in God's kingdom.

Serve and Protect

This is humanity's priestly vocation.

We are priests in the temple of God. Though English translations often given an agricultural feel to these Hebrew verbs, like "till it and keep it" (Gen. 2:15), Ellen Davis (among others) has demonstrated that this is priestly language.[1] When these two words occur together elsewhere in the Hebrew Bible, they describe the Levitical service of God's appointed servants in the tabernacle (Num. 3:7–8; 8:26; 18:7).

The first verb normally describes ministering or serving the ground (Gen. 2:5; 3:23; 4:2, 12) or the garden (Gen. 2:15). The second verb is normally translated as "keep," "guard," or "protect." Priests protect or guard the holiness of the sanctuary. This may include agricultural dimensions, but given the temple and sanctuary language in Genesis 1–2, it stresses humanity's priestly role within creation. Like priests in the temple, we serve God's creation and protect it from anything unclean.

As priests, we mediate the praise of creation to the Creator, and we mediate God's rule over the world in creation. We represent creation in our praise of God, and we fill the material world with thanksgiving as we receive creation from God with gratitude. As priests, we bless creation and lead creation in blessing God.

Priests are deeply connected with the parties they mediate. As images of God, we represent God to creation. As part of creation, we represent creation to God. We are spiritual-material beings who participate in both the spiritual reality of God and the material reality of creation. This is part of our human identity.

Our shared materiality with creation binds us together as community. Materiality, rather than discarded in the end, is designed as a means by which creatures participate in the life of God. Creation is not an addendum to humanity but constitutive. We are creatures bound by our creaturehood. Neither finitude nor materiality is evil—they are good.

Together, humanity and nature are creation. One without the other is less than the goodness God created. Together, humanity and nature declare the glory of God. This is the goodness God created, and the created reality praises God. Together, humanity and nature mediate the presence of God within creation. The material world is sacramental, a true means of grace.

When we confess materiality as a means of communion between humanity and God, we affirm its value, meaning, and significance. We affirm the inherent spirituality of materiality itself. Materiality is not a temporary measure for testing humanity in some sort of probationary period. On the contrary, materiality is designed as the means through which the transcendent God encounters humanity.

We live as embodied, material persons who engage other embodied, material persons within the material creation itself. This is where we live. We live out our human vocation in the nitty-gritty grind of daily life. We work, play, and love with and through our bodies, and we encounter God through eating and drinking at tables, walking and working in the fields, and building and creating in our work. Spirituality and materiality are integral dimensions of the authentic human experience. One without the other is incomplete—indeed, they are ultimately one.

God's House Vandalized

> *Because humanity sinned,*
> *cursed is the ground because of you,*
> *in toil you shall eat of it all the days of your life;*
> *thorns and thistles it shall bring froth for you;*
> *and you shall eat the plants of the field.*
> *By the sweat of your face*
> *you shall eat bread*
> *until you return to the ground,*
> *for out of it you were taken;*
> *you are dust, and to dust you shall return.*
> —Gen. 3:17b–19

"Curse" language appears twice in Genesis 3. The first is applied to the serpent, which represents chaos, including death (Gen. 3:14), and the second is quoted above. "Curse," due to the expulsion from Eden, now characterizes creation. Outside of Eden, without the tree of life, anxiety and death reign. While everything was put under humanity's feet in Eden (Ps. 8:6), now death reigns over humanity and terrorizes it (Heb. 2:8–9).

Eden was vandalized when humanity listened to the serpent and chose autonomy over submission, choosing death over life. Expelled from Eden, God's sanctuary, humanity now faced chaos, anxiety, and death. They were thrown into the chaos Eden was designed to subdue. Eden, in effect, was removed from the earth, and humanity was exiled to chaos. They lost *shalom*, peace, and wholeness.

This represented a number of "losses." Not only did they lose intimacy with God; they experienced the loss of intimacy with each other. Whatever the meaning of Genesis 3:16, it describes an emerging tension between men and women. Once partners in creation, they are now combatants.

Humanity also experienced the loss of *shalom* with creation. In Eden, humanity blessed and named the animals, shared food, and lived with them in peaceful relationship. Ejected from Eden, they encounter the chaotic "tooth and claw" world that existed outside of Eden—the world humanity was designed to "subdue" (order) but will now battle. Humanity now struggles with creation, subject to death as creation itself is enslaved to death.

Genesis 4–11 describes the degenerative tumble of humanity into chaos. Instead of subduing it, they increased the chaos. Cain killed Abel (Gen. 4:8), and subsequently the earth was "filled with violence" (Gen. 6:11, 13). Violence characterized "all flesh," and consequently God determined to destroy "all flesh," including "the earth" (Gen. 6:13). Though God cleansed the earth with destructive waters—a form of "uncreation" for the sake of re-creation—chaos and violence returned after the flood and reached its zenith in Babel's arrogance. There humanity—in parody of God's own self-counsel in Genesis 1:26—said to itself, "Let us make a name for ourselves," and they built a *ziggurat*, or "temple" (Gen. 11:4). Instead of living in God's temple as God's royal priests, they created their own temple in order to "make a name" for themselves. Such human arrogance is at the root of sin as well as the suffering of the earth.

Barred from Eden, humanity was subjected to chaos, symbolized by the serpent, darkness, the waters, and death. However, God will *reverse the curse.* In the new heavens and new earth, there is no more curse (Rev. 22:3). There is no more sea, which represents chaos (Rev. 21:1). There is no more darkness (Rev. 22:5), and there is no more death (Rev. 21:4).

God will redeem creation from its curse and renew its life and purpose. In the end, God will liberate creation from its bondage and resurrect it from its corruption, just as God raised Jesus from the dead and will raise us from the grave to live upon a new earth under a new heaven.

In the end, God will once again dwell upon the earth with humanity (Rev. 21:3).

CONCLUSION

Creation is centered on God rather than on humanity or biology. In other words, the world is God-centered rather than human-centered or life-centered. Creation is God's design—God's home—and we are God's royal priests who care for God's good creation as our divinely gifted ministry.

In the end, creation will again become a cathedral of praise, and God's *shalom* will fill it.

BULLET POINTS

- God built a house in which to make a home with humanity, and it is called "creation."
- God entered into a partnership with humanity to cocreate with God—to multiply and fill the cosmos, subdue the remaining chaos within it, shepherd its growth and development, and protect it from harm.
- Through human sin, creation was bound to death and corruption, which God will reverse through resurrection.

QUESTIONS

1. What are some ethical implications embedded in the claim, "Creation is God's house"? How do we live differently within creation from that perspective?

2. What aspects of God's partnership with humanity—the vocation given to humanity—resonate with your experience or challenge you to participate in that vocation? How does your career participate in that partnership?

3. In what ways are you called to "reverse the curse" that burdens creation? How do you presently participate in God's redemptive goal for creation through your life and work?

CHAPTER THREE

"Praise Him, Sun and Moon"

Creation and Its Praise of God in Psalms

*The universe is, itself, the offspring of God's love.
It was not created simply because he had the wisdom
and power to do it. The element of love entered
into the intention, characterized the execution,
and approved the completion of his labors.*

—Alexander Campbell[1]

The psalter is the Spirit-inspired temple of the Bible, a literary Holy of Holies. For three thousand years, the psalms have been the heart of worship—corporate and private—in Israel and the church. Entering this literary sanctuary is a full sensory experience for the worshipper. Laced with the grittiness of life and the grandeur of God, as we step into this holy place we smell incense, see hands raised in boisterous praise amid the gathered congregation, and hear the cries of lament. In the psalms, the same Spirit who breathed life upon the earth inspires holistic worship, which embodies the great commandment to love God with our minds, souls, and bodies (Deut. 6:4–5; Matt. 22:34–35) as we join the cosmos in worship. All creation sings the Lord's praise.

Psalms opens up a fuller vision of reality. This sanctuary of praise and prayer invokes the world in which God reigns. In psalms, through worship, God gives Israel eyes to see and ears to hear what God is doing in the world. Immersion in this worldview—constructed in God-centered worship—invites us to embrace God's purpose for creation and the beauty of creation as a reflection of God's glory, and to find our own place within creation to lead heaven and earth in the worship of the Creator.

For God So Loves the World

The world envisioned in worship enables God's people to interpret the cosmos in the light of God's claims, purpose, and mission. It reframes pain and injustice and draws attention to love, beauty, and justice. If you ask an Israelite fresh from pilgrimage to the temple, "How do you know God loves you?" she might say something like, "I know God loves me because God created the world and redeemed Israel." Lifting her hands to heaven, she would burst into song: "O give thanks to the LORD, for he is good, for his steadfast love endures forever" (Ps. 136:1). What is the evidence for this radical claim? The answer appears in worship. God is the one,

> who alone does great wonders,
> for his steadfast love endures forever;
> who by understanding made the heavens,
> for his steadfast love endures forever;
> who spread out the earth on the waters,
> for his steadfast love endures forever;
> who made the great lights,
> for his steadfast love endures forever;

> *the sun to rule over the day,*
> *for his steadfast love endures forever;*
> *the moon and the stars to rule over the night,*
> *for his steadfast love endures forever. (Ps. 136:4–9)*

God's first act of love is not the cross or even the grace of the Exodus. Creation is God's first loving act. Inhabiting the sanctuary of worship, Israel sees "nature" around it through the eyes of wonder rather than utilitarianism. Nature is, in fact, transformed into creation. The physical universe reflects the warmth and love of Jesus's Father.

Psalm 33 elaborates the character and work of the Lord of Israel. God is described in vivid ways:

> *For the word of the LORD is upright,*
> *and all his work is done in faithfulness.*
> *He loves righteousness and justice;*
> *the earth is full of the steadfast love of the LORD. (Ps. 33:4–5)*

What is this faithful, righteous, and loving work? Sometimes it is saving people from sin or delivering the poor, but not in Psalm 33. Instead, it is the creation of the universe. "By the word of the LORD the heavens were made, and all their host by the breath of his mouth" (Ps. 33:6). The beginning of the steadfast love of the Lord is not deliverance from sin or oppression but the creation of the cosmos. Indeed, it is an act of "justice." No wonder the psalm declares, "The earth is full of the steadfast love of the LORD" (Ps. 33:5).

Creation is more than a showcase of God's power. God is an artist who cares for, tends to, protects, and loves this world. Psalm 104 is formally linked to Psalm 103 with its breathtaking vistas of God's steadfast love, which is higher than the heavens (Ps. 103:11).

This love, manifested in God's "works" (Ps. 103:22), ushers us into a magnificent meditation upon God's steadfast love for all creation.

Reveling in the diversity of creation, Psalm 104 checks the arrogant assumption that the world exists primarily for human use and purposes. God has other concerns besides humans, and it places us as one among many inhabitants of the earth who receive the gift of life from the Creator. The psalm pictures Yahweh clothed in majesty, building a cosmic temple in which to dwell (Ps. 78:69; Isa. 40:22). Next it casts a beatific vision of earth, mentioned seven times (Ps. 104:5, 9, 13, 14, 24, 32, 35), and centers on the rich diversity of life filling it. The psalmist celebrates God's loving care for the world: "You make springs gush forth in the valleys; they flow between the hills" (Ps. 104:10). This "drink is [for] every wild animal" (Ps. 104:11). The birds, who "sing among the branches" (Ps. 104:12), benefit, and the earth itself is "satisfied with the fruit of your work" (Ps. 104:13). Humans are not even listed among the beneficiaries of divine hydration.

The Lord's hands-on approach to tending creation means God also feeds life. Humans finally enter the picture. Having satisfied the earth with water, God provides horticulture for animals to eat and viniculture for humans to drink. As water blesses the animals and wine refreshes humans, so now the Creator abundantly cares for "trees of the LORD" (Ps. 104:14–16).

The psalmist again confesses the marvelous manner of divine provision for the nonhuman world. The "trees of the LORD" are not simply for human use. Rather, the trees were created for birds (Ps. 104:16–17). The majestic mountains are "for the wild goats" (Ps. 104:18).

One of the inspired poet's most startling claims is that humans are not the only ones who work hours and punch the clock. Both animals and humans share the world but are separated by temporal domains (Ps. 104:19–23). The sun and moon is creation's clock (Gen. 1:14–18). The animals in the forests and on the mountains work for a living under the cover of the darkness, while humans seek their livelihood under the sun. Lions work the midnight shift and, like their fellow human creatures, get their earnings from God (Ps. 104:21; cf. Job 38:39–41). After binding all creatures together under the sun and moon, the congregation bursts out in awe-filled worship:

> O LORD, how manifold are your works!
> In wisdom you have made them all;
> the earth is full of your creatures. (Ps. 104:24)

God showers steadfast love on humans, lions, birds, goats, and trees. But human eyes have never seen some of God's most amazing creatures. One creature, called Leviathan, lives in God's aquarium, the vast sea. God created Leviathan to frolic and play in the deep! It lives carefree (Ps. 104:26).

The psalmist concludes this cosmic panorama with all creation—small and great, nonhuman and human—brought together as contingent creatures utterly dependent upon the grace of God:

> These all look to you to give them their food in due season;
> when you give to them, they gather it up;
> when you open your hand, they are filled with good things.
> When you hide your face, they are dismayed;
> when you take away their breath they die and return to dust.
> When you send forth your Spirit, they are created;
> and you renew the face of the ground. (Ps. 104:27–30)

Here is the death knell to Deism. God's hands-on approach to creation is a continuous action. As the preacher says, the universe is "sustained" by divine grace (Heb. 1:3). Here, as in the initial creation itself (Gen. 1:2; 2:7), God's Spirit gives life to all. When life appears—whether it is human, animal, or vegetation—a profound miracle has taken place. Perhaps Jesus has these words in mind when he remembers how God clothes the grass of the field and adorns the lilies with beauty. Our Father feeds ravens and even notices the death of a sparrow (Matt. 6:25–34). No wonder the psalmist is awed. May we recover that sense of wonder!

According to the last five verses, humanity is not the only one who delights in creation. Bathed in gracious "glory," the Lord is called to rejoice, to take pleasure in creation: "May the glory of the LORD endure forever; may the LORD rejoice in his works" (Ps. 104:31). This asks God to continue a love affair with creation. In Genesis, the Creator announces the goodness of the world, and in Psalm 104, God delights in it.

Psalm 104 is a gentle but firm check on human arrogance. Through a misreading of other texts (e.g., Gen. 1:28), we sometimes assume the cosmos was placed here for us. But Genesis already told us the world was "good" when it was inhabited only by fish, birds, and trees—before a single human appeared. God is the caretaker of the garden, and humans are only one of God's wonderful creatures in this psalm. Both animals and humans receive sustenance from the same divine source. In Psalm 104, God is an artist who creates for beauty and joy as well as utility.

God the Creator and God the Provider are linked through the work of the Holy Spirit. If all life is created, nourished, and loved by God, then there are more ways to grieve the Spirit of life than there is a lack of personal sanctification. How we respond to the majestic love of God in creation is a response to God's Spirit. To treat what God so lavishly loves cavalierly grieves the Spirit.

Above all, Psalm 104 reveals an astounding truth: creation, animate and inanimate, is the object of divine love. If God, like an artist, dotes so tenderly over it, then should not those created in God's image reflect the same divine delight, love, and care for creation? This is, in part, what biblical "dominion" means.

Creation's Praise of the Creator God

In the world encountered in worship, we not only gain a proper perspective on our place in creation and God's continual loving work; we also learn we are not alone in the sanctuary. Everything in creation worships the Creator, except some human beings. Isaiah, turning choir director, commands:

> *Sing, O heavens, for the LORD has done it;*
> *shout, O depths of the earth;*
> *break forth into singing, O mountains,*
> *O forest, and every tree in it! (Isa 44:23)*

Creation explodes in worship because the children of God are redeemed: "For the LORD has redeemed Jacob" (Isa. 44:23b). This is precisely what creation is waiting for in Paul's climactic text in Romans. Creation is "eagerly longing for the revealing of the children of God" (Rom. 8:19). Redemption serves creation, and creation in turn worships the creating and redeeming God.

Worship is not only an embodied, full sensory experience; it is a full creation experience. Before Psalm 24 identifies who may ascend the "holy hill of worship" (Ps. 24:3), it reminds us that "the earth is the LORD's and all that is in it" (Ps. 24:1). This is the ground of worship, and it offends modernity. In worship, we are confronted with this humbling fact: everything belongs to God. As priests of creation, we step forward to lead creation in the worship of the Creator. Like Psalm 104, the psalter as a whole moves to a crescendo of all-out worship. A whole orchestra meets us in Psalm 148:2–13:

> *Praise him, all his angels,*
> *praise him, all his host!*
> *Praise him, sun and moon;*
> *praise him, all you shining stars!*
> *Praise him, you highest heavens!*
>
> *Let them praise the name of the* Lord,
> *for he commanded and they were created.*
> *He established them forever and ever;*
> *he fixed their bounds, which cannot be passed.*
>
> *Praise the* Lord *from the earth,*
> *you sea monsters and all deeps,*
> *fire and hail, snow and frost,*
> *snowy wind fulfilling his command!*
>
> *Mountains and all hills,*
> *fruit trees and all cedars!*
> *Wild animals and all cattle,*
> *creepy things and flying birds!*
>
> *Kings of the earth and all peoples,*
> *princes and all rulers of the earth!*
> *Young men and women alike*
> *old and young together!*
>
> *Let them praise the name of the* Lord
> *for his name is exalted:*
> *his glory is above earth and heaven.*

Many react to this breathtaking cosmic spectacle with doubt and even disbelief. Some are offended if their worship is not more valuable than the creepy crawlies' (rodents, reptiles, and insects). Yet Psalm 148 reflects a pervasive theme in Scripture. We must resist "domesticating the text" in order that we might be shaped by its concerns.[2] The text gives us "eyes to see and ears to hear."

The psalmist, as cosmic priest, exhorts the cosmos to praise the Lord, complete with a checklist of worshipers moving from the heavens (Ps. 148:1–6) to the earth with its various creatures, humans among them (Ps. 148:7–12). Animals, including "sea monsters" (Ps. 148:7), are commanded to add their voice to the chorus that bears witness to the glory of the Lord.

These calls to worship express praise. They reflect the range of God's works and, therefore, God's praiseworthiness. The roll call of creatures suggests both their individuality and their complementary nature. Each has its own distinctiveness and function. Just as French horns, trumpets, cellos, and violins blend their individualities together to create symphonic music, so does God's creation. Every creature, like each instrument fulfilling its role, blends together in profound harmony for the praise of the Lord God. Isaiah 42:10–11 brings humanity and cosmos together in this same manner:

> *Sing to the LORD a new song,*
> *his praise to the end of the earth!*
> *Let the sea roar and all that fills it,*
> *the coastlands and their inhabitants.*
> *Let the desert and its towns lift up their voice,*
> *the villages that Kedar inhabits;*
> *let the inhabitants of Sela sing for joy,*
> *let them shout from the tops of the mountains. (NRSV)*

Humans may not mind being compared to angels (Ps. 148:2) but wouldn't like sharing praise with bugs. Worship reminds us we are creatures, something we have resisted since our expulsion from Eden. Just as Psalm 104 reveals we are "brethren" with the trees and animals, so Psalm 148 reveals our worship is simply part of theirs. We join creation in the song it is already singing! The exuberant praise of Psalm 148 *is* that revelation, often unheard and unrecognized by humans whose vision of the world is out of sorts.

This language is not limited to some sort of "primitive" pre-Christian age of spirituality. John the Prophet reports the outburst of creation's praise and, much like Psalm 148, combines angelic, human, and animal voices:

> *Then I looked, and I heard the voice of many angels surrounding the throne and the living creatures and the elders; they numbered myriads of myriads and thousands of thousands, singing with full voice,*
>
> > *"Worthy is the Lamb that was slaughtered*
> > *to receive power and wealth and wisdom and might*
> > *and honor and glory and blessing!"*
>
> *Then I heard every creature in heaven and on earth and under the earth and in the sea, and all that is in them, singing,*
>
> > *"To the one seated on the throne and to the Lamb*
> > *be blessing and honor and glory and might forever and ever!"*
>
> *And the four living creatures said, "Amen!" And the elders fell down and worshipped. (Rev. 5:11–14 NRSV)*

The world invoked in Psalm 148 reveals how deeply God is connected to the earth.

We realize psalms use poetic and metaphorical language, and we do not intend to abuse such language. However, metaphors are still true. Indeed, metaphors often convey some truth more effectively than prose. To put it another way, there are continuities between rocks, eagles, mothers, fathers, and God. The worship of creation, metaphorical it may be, nevertheless says something true about the relationship between God and creation. Leading creation in worship, humanity connects God and creation with the language of praise and calls humanity into a proper relationship with creation.

CONCLUSION

Creation responds to the call of God. Creatures turn to God (Ps. 104:21; 145:15–16). God, in turn, responds with steadfast love and care (Ps. 147:9). Praise reflects God's honor and glory back to God, and it bears witness to what God has done. Among the purposes of creation is praise. When lived out, it is directed to the Creator.

BULLET POINTS

- Psalms reminds us how intimately humanity is bound to God's good creation.
- Creation both displays God's powerful love and is the object of God's steadfast love.
- In worship, we join a chorus already singing. As priests, we lead creation in the praise of God.

QUESTIONS

1. How might our discussion of the psalms impact your
    reading of John 3:16? What does it mean for God to love
    creation?

2. Where and how do you see God's loving care for nonhu-
    man creation? How does science give us insight into this
    loving care?

3. How might our leading and sharing worship with creation
    impact our congregational experiences?

CHAPTER FOUR

Wisdom and Creation

Delight in Beauty, Agony in Chaos

Can't you feel it in your bones?
Something isn't right here
Something that you've always known
But you don't know why
But when you see the morning sun
Burning through a silver mist
Don't you want to thank someone?
Don't you want to thank someone for this?

—Andrew Peterson, "Don't You Want to Thank Someone?"

The wisdom literature of the Hebrew Bible is solidly rooted in a theology of creation. God's creation gives rise to wisdom, shaping the rhythm of living well within God's world. Yet chaos disrupts this order, and Hebrew wisdom acknowledges that frustrating reality.

On the one hand, Proverbs and the Song of Songs delight in creation's order. On the other hand, Ecclesiastes and Job struggle with how to live in a creation where chaos is so unruly and unpredictable. Wisdom, in either case, has a word for humanity.

Wisdom Affirms the Goodness of Creation

Proverbs and the Song of Songs revel in the joy of creation, delighting in its goodness. Proverbs lives by the wisdom embedded within God's created order, and the Song of Songs playfully celebrates human sexuality as part of God's good order.

Wisdom Creates and Delights

God created "in the beginning" through wisdom, and wisdom is interwoven into the fabric of the world's life. Both threads run through Proverbs.

Wisdom, personified as a woman, frames the book of Proverbs. Proverbs 1–9 and the poem about the sage woman of Proverbs 31 are connected. Both women are the concrete embodiment of living wisely and harmoniously within God's good creation.

Lady Wisdom demands to be heard in the public square:

> *Does not wisdom call out?*
> *Does not understanding raise her voice?*
> *At the highest point along the way,*
> *where the paths meet, she takes her stand;*
> *beside the gate leading into the city,*
> *at the entrance she cries aloud. (Prov. 8:1–3 NIV)*

Humans, as the book's proverbial sayings demonstrate, tend to use power in godless ways. Kings abuse subjects, the rich steal from the poor, lips utter deceit, and God's good gifts of sex, wine, and food are perverted. Consequently, Lady Wisdom aims her sermon at "all that live" (Prov. 8:4). From her, people learn faithful ways to live:

> *I walk in the way of righteousness,*
> *along the paths of justice,*

> *bestowing a rich inheritance on those who love me*
> *and making their treasuries full. (Prov. 8:20–21 NIV)*

Lady Wisdom is the secret to life under sun because God used her to create the world, and wisdom has sown her DNA throughout creation:

> *The LORD brought me forth as the first of his works,*
> *before his deeds of old;*
> *I was formed long ages ago,*
> *at the very beginning, when the world came to be.*
>
> *I was there when he set the heavens in place,*
> *when he marked out the horizon on the face of the deep,*
> *when he established the clouds above*
> *and fixed securely the fountains of the deep,*
> *when he gave the sea its boundary so the waters would not*
> *   overstep his command,*
> *and when he marked out the foundations of the earth.*
> *Then I was constantly at his side.*
> *I was filled with delight day after day,*
> *rejoicing always in his presence,*
> *rejoicing in his whole world*
> *and delighting in mankind. (Prov. 8:22–23, 27–31 NIV)*

God's own wisdom is displayed in creation. Wisdom was present at—and was even the inspiration for—creation.

Lady Wisdom, the master worker, is God's own delight. She rejoices "before" God, celebrating God's magnificent "inhabited world" and delighting in "the human race." Some suggest Lady Wisdom is a personified idea of creation itself. God, therefore, rejoices in creation.

Lady Wisdom concludes her sermon by urging people to come
and learn her ways (Prov. 8:32–36). When they listen to her, they
will find life and "favor" from the Lord (Prov. 8:34–36). As the
source of creation, wisdom is the art of living together in harmony
with both creation and the community inhabiting God's world.
Consequently, wisdom celebrates the wonder of God's creation:

> *Three things are too wonderful for me;*
> *four I do not understand:*
> *the way of an of an eagle in the sky,*
> *the way of a snake on a rock,*
> *the way of a ship on the high seas,*
> *the way of a man with a girl. (Prov. 30:18–19 NRSV)*

Ships, snakes, birds, and sex—four wonders within God's creation.
Each expresses a world filled with divine wisdom. Humans share in
that wisdom when they live in harmony with the wisdom embedded in God's good creation.

Delighting in Our Humanity

No biblical book has suffered at the hands of Platonic dualism
among Christians as much as the Song of Songs. Jewish sages,
however, hailed the Song as the "Holy of Holies" of Scripture. The
Song envisions a world in which fractured human beings return
to the temple of God to experience the delights of intimacy in
the Garden of Eden. The song rejoices in the gift of being human.

There are many connections between the song and the first
three chapters of Genesis. In the Garden of Eden, the Bible remembers a paradisiacal world of love, *shalom*, and mutuality without
shame. This beautiful world was vandalized—even raped. The historical world of Israel, like ours, is a post-Eden world searching

for intimacy. The "symphony of love" begun in Eden became a "cacophony of abuse" in the chaos outside of Eden.

The Song of Songs redeems that symphony of love. In the song, God calls us back to Eden to enjoy the most holy relationship known to humanity. In the sexual relationship, the song loudly and proudly proclaims Paradise regained. Even now, the song suggests, we can experience Eden in our relationships. The song does not portray the couple in the poem as the "first couple" from Genesis; it is deeply aware that we live in a world filled with broken relationships. However, in the song, the woman and the man rediscover Edenic values in the most intimate dimension of their relationship. They relish one another.

The song flows via dialogue between the woman and the man, the woman and the daughters of Jerusalem, and the woman and the night guards. The dialogue's distribution is far from equal. She is the primary speaker; approximately 70 percent of the words come from her mouth. The woman is the primary "actor" in the poem and the book's dominant personality. She carries the dialogue (eighty-one out of one hundred thirty verses).

The man often praises her (Song 1:9–11, 15; 2:2; 4:1–7; 6:4–9; 7:2–10), yet his voice disappears completely by chapter eight. Even when he comes to "his garden," it is only at her invitation (Song 4:16–5:1a).

Like Lady Wisdom, she is not passive! She sets the agenda. For example, she outdoes his praises for her by bragging about him (Song 1:16–17; 2:3). She *begins* the song and she *ends* the song. She is the one who speaks its refrains. She is the one who calls on her lover to do things, including draw her after him (Song 1:4), be like a gazelle (Song 2:17), come out to the fields with her (Song 7:12–14), set her as a seal on his arm (Song 8:6), and to flee with her (Song

8:14). She seeks him (Song 1:7). She "seizes" him to bring him into the chamber of love (Song 3:4; 8:1–2). She is such a powerful presence the man is driven mad by just one of her glances (Song 4:9).

The Song of Songs is egalitarian, representing a complete subversion of the values of the cursed world in Genesis 3. The egalitarian note is sung in 2:16: "My beloved is mine and I am his!" The restoration of Eden is evoked when she exclaims, "I am my lover's and his desire [*tesugah*] is for me" (Song 7:10). This echoes Genesis 3:16: "Your desire [*tesugah*] will be for your husband." In the relationship as God created and desires it, the song celebrates the mutuality of their joyful love. Healing human intimacy finds a world recreated:

> *My beloved speaks to me:*
> *"Arise, my love, my fair one,*
> *and come away;*
> *for now the winter is past,*
> *the rain is over and gone.*
> *The flowers appear on the earth;*
> *the time of singing has come,*
> *and the voice of the turtledove*
> *is heard in our land.*
> *The fig tree put forth its figs,*
> *and the vines are in blossom;*
> *they give forth fragrance.*
> *Arise, my love, my fair one,*
> *and come away." (Song 2:10–13)*

The springtime is the crux of the "argument." The flowering of spring is the reason she steals away with him. Spring is for gardens. Gardens are for the couple and their enjoyment. The world is not merely useful; it is enjoyed.

It is good to be human. The passion we have for one another and God's creation reflects God's own love. At the climax of the Song of Songs, the woman sings:

> *For Love is as strong as death,*
> *passion as fierce as the grave;*
> *The flash of it is a flash of fire,*
> *a flame of Yahweh* [salhebetyah] *himself! (Song 8:6; our translation)*

When Creation Frustrates

The "tooth and claw" of creation as well as its tragic effect on human life is frustrating. Israel's wisdom literature not only emphasizes the goodness of creation; it also laments its absurdity and heartbreaking reality.

Life Is Absurd and Good

Living within God's creation is both frustrating and delightful. Qoheleth, the teacher in Ecclesiastes, offers an extended reflection on this conundrum.

Life is absurd. The word *hebel* describes this frustration, and Qoheleth uses it thirty-seven times (cf. Eccl. 1:2). Literally it means "vapor"—like a breath in cold air—and thus communicates brevity. Metaphorically it means "vanity," signifying the seeming pointlessness of life.

The word, however, has more punch than this. It encompasses the unfathomable nature of life, the deep impenetrable mystery of life and death. Some suggest "enigma," and life is enigmatic because we simply do not know. We are limited in perspective and we cannot make sense of life.

Some suggest "absurd." The seemingly ceaseless, circular, and pointless merry-go-round of life has no goal, meaning, or worth. Life, because of death, is hauntingly absurd.

Genesis 1–11 lies behind Ecclesiastes. When Qoheleth probes life, the teacher evokes the narrative world of Abel (the same word as *hebel*). The seemingly pointless, absurd, and unjust death of Abel at the hands of Cain symbolizes human existence in a world enslaved to death. Our lives are like Abel's.

We must sit with the teacher for a season rather than move on too quickly. Sometimes we are forced to do so when chaos assaults human life. We recoil at the death of children in tornadoes. We are shocked when children are killed in school shootings. Terrorists assault innocents in Kenya, Syria, Lebanon, Iraq, Paris, and on Russian airliners. Sometimes all we can do is agree with Qoheleth: "Everything is absolutely absurd!" And in those times, it is difficult to imagine joy again.

Paul highlights this *hebel* when he uses the Septuagint's Greek translation of *hebel*: "The creation was subjected to *futility*" (Rom. 8:20). Paul recognizes the frustration of creation's present condition, which enslaves creation and, consequently, affirms Qoheleth's own observation. Creation laments the agony of death just as humanity does.

Yet, without forgetting life is *hebel*, Qoheleth also confesses that God has endowed creation with joy and value. Though disoriented by the absurdity of life, Qoheleth remembers the Creator (12:1, 6) and "knows that whatever God does endures forever" (3:14). Qoheleth holds these two truths in tension: life is absurd and God is the Creator. Holding these in tension, Qoheleth confesses no one knows "the work of God, who makes everything" (11:5). Life is an enigma.

Though life is filled with futility, we also experience goodness, and somehow and in some way, God gives joy in the midst of absurdity. Ecclesiastes states, "I know that there is nothing better for them than to be happy and enjoy themselves as long as they live; moreover, it is God's gift that all should eat and drink and take pleasure in their toil" (3:12–13 NRSV). In addition, it says, "Likewise, all to whom God gives wealth and possessions and whom he enables to enjoy them, and to accept their lot and find enjoyment in their toil—this is the gift of God" (5:19 NRSV). It also says, "Go, eat your bread with enjoyment, and drink your wine with a merry heart; for God has long ago approved what you do . . . Enjoy life with your wife" (9:7, 9 NRSV).

Qoheleth, while observing the absurdity of life, believes the Hebrew story. As Creator, God shares many good gifts with humanity and invites humanity to enjoy them. Though labor has become "toil," people may yet find joy in their work or the vocation God gave humanity in the beginning. Though wealth is often used to oppress others, people may yet enjoy it as God's gift. Though many may abuse both wine and spouses, they are nevertheless God's good gifts.

Life is both *hebel* and filled with the Creator's gifts. We lament and recognize the absurdity of human existence, but we also receive God's gifts with gratitude and joy. Though we feel the tragic traumas deep within our souls, we still laugh and enjoy God's good gifts, and this is part of the absurdity of life in the present creation. Qoheleth does not reject God's creation. Instead, he cries out for the full realization of God's reign within it.

The Hand of God

Job, like Qoheleth, knew the absurdity of life. Because what he feared most had happened (Job 3:25), Job believed he would "never again see good" in the flesh (Job 7:7). Job fully experienced *hebel*, losing his children to death and his prosperity to theft. He concluded God had become his enemy (Job 30:16–23).

Job is frustrated with God because he holds God responsible for his circumstances. God is sovereign—God reigns over creation and, consequently, Job knows God has had a "hand" in what has happened to him. If anyone doubts this, Job argues, they should ask creation itself:

> But ask the animals, and they will teach you;
> the birds of the air, and they will teach you;
> ask the plants of the earth, and they will teach you;
> and the fish of the sea will declare to you.
> Who among all these does not know
> that the hand of the LORD has done this?
> In his hand is the life of every living thing
> and the breath of every human being. (Job 12:7–10)

Not only do we hear echoes of Genesis 1; we also recognize how the "hand of the LORD" reaffirms Yahweh's involvement in Job's suffering—Yahweh extended a "hand" to permit the accuser to test Job (1:11; 2:5). All life and breath is in the "hand" of God.

Given Job's confession of God as Creator, two images, among many, communicate Job's frustration. First, Job believes God views him as a chaotic threat to God's creation and, consequently, God has targeted him (7:20). Job asks, "Am I the Sea, or the Dragon that you set a guard over me?" (7:12). Second, given God's treatment, Job believes God has neglected him just as wild animals in the desert are marginalized by God (so he thinks) and ignored by human beings: "I am a brother of jackals, and a companion of ostriches," Job complains (30:29). He is no longer the object of God's loving care, just like the desert animals.

Interestingly, God addresses both metaphors when he encounters Job (38:1). In the initial speech (38:2–39:30), Yahweh reminds

Job how divine wisdom created the cosmos (38:36–37), and then describes Yahweh's relationship with the wild desert animals, including lions, ravens, mountain goats, wild donkeys, wild oxen, and the ostrich (39:13–18), which receives the most attention. "Job," Yahweh says, "I love the ostrich, and I care for it, just like I love and care for you!"

In the second speech, Yahweh reminds Job how God created the Behemoth (Job 40:15–24) and Leviathan (Job 41:1–34). These animals represent chaotic forces within creation.[1] Chaos exists within God's creation, but they are not God's enemies. In fact, God has endowed these animals with majestic features. Yet God rules over them. Chaos does not threaten God, and God will ultimately remove chaos from creation in the new heaven and new earth. "Job," Yahweh says, "I control the chaos, and the chaos in your life has neither dethroned me nor has it disrupted my love for you. I love my creation, and even chaos has its purpose within it."

The book of Job confesses God is sovereign over creation, and even chaos serves God's purposes. God loves and cares for everything within creation, including wild animals and Job.

CONCLUSION

Biblical wisdom is founded on God's good creation. The splendor of the trees, oceans, skies, and humans proclaim the glory of divine wisdom. At the same time, wisdom knows chaos exists within this good creation, and it is exacerbated by human rebellion, which creates more chaos. Lady Wisdom and the Song of Songs proclaim, "Creation is good; being human is good." Qoheleth and the story of Job testify to our need for redemption from agonizing chaos. Consequently, we remember our Creator, lament the chaos in our lives, trust in God's wisdom, and enjoy God's gifts.

BULLET POINTS

- Wisdom is woven into the fabric of creation and life under the sun.
- Wisdom affirms the intrinsic goodness of the world amid the agony of chaos.
- We live harmoniously with creation when we embrace God's wisdom.

QUESTIONS

1. How does wisdom affirm human existence as a gift of grace?

2. How is "wonder" a requirement for living peacefully (*shalom*) within God's creation?

3. How have you experienced the "agony of chaos" in your life? What has wisdom taught you in such experiences, especially in how we compassionately relate to others in the throes of such agony?

CHAPTER FIVE

Dreams of Eden

Death and Resurrection in the Prophets

*The creation and fall of Adam and Eve are the first acts
in the drama, ending in the resurrection and redemption
of the faithful in the more than restored paradise
of God pictured in the last chapter of Revelation.*

—David Lipscomb[1]

The new world the Hebrew prophets imagine is a renewed Eden. Though the earth is presently ravaged by chaos, sin, and evil powers, a "new heaven and new earth" will emerge through God's redemptive power—a new creation (Isa. 65:17–25).

Genesis 1–11 narrates the story of the world. God made it good. God made royal priests from the earth to share in the care and expansion of Eden. But they rebelled. Once characterized by *shalom*, Eden experienced cataclysmic vandalism. Bound together in creation, the earth and earthlings became bound together in corruption.

Humanity's expulsion from Eden resulted in further degradation. What was created "very good" had become "corrupt in God's sight" (Gen. 6:11). It was not just humanity but the earth itself that was corrupted with human sin. God took the drastic measure of unleashing the flood upon the world. Once again, humanity and the world were bound together again in corruption, destruction, and salvation. God goes through a lot of trouble to make sure a priestly family and animals are redeemed together.

In the flood narrative, the Creator does not abandon creation's purpose. God resurrects creation and enters a unilateral covenant of grace. This everlasting covenant is made with humans and "with every living creature," including "the birds, domestic animals, and every animal of the earth" (Gen. 9:10). The covenant, like the act of creation itself, is unconditional. Here, at the beginning of the Bible, we learn the hope of the world rests with God.

The story of Israel is the story of humanity. The story of the Promised Land is the story of the world. Abraham's family is chosen as God's instrument for healing the nations. They are placed in the world as royal priests (Ex. 19:5–6), and God dwells among them in the midst of the world. But Israel failed in her lofty calling, and she was expelled from the land and God's presence. And the land lamented.

The Hope of Israel

God reigns over creation, and creation is the Creator's loyal servant. For example, Yahweh's sovereignty over land and sea is evident throughout the small book of Jonah. Creation is Yahweh's instrument of "severe mercy" toward Jonah. God hurls a mighty wind upon the sea to create a storm (Jon. 1:4), calms the sea (Jon. 1:15), and provides a great fish (Jon. 1:17), a shady bush (Jon. 4:6), and a small worm (Jon. 4:7). God pursues Jonah through creation for the sake of salvation—it is not punishment. God even saves the animals in Nineveh as they participate in the city's repentance (Jon. 3:6–8)! Yahweh, the maker of land and sea, uses creation for God's own purposes and intends to redeem it along with humanity, as Jonah's mission to Nineveh illustrates.

The fate of creation—its worshiping, lamenting, and redemption—is deeply intertwined with humanity. When the patience of Yahweh is exhausted and judgment falls upon God's covenant people, we find echoes of the primeval narrative. Amos, the earliest-writing prophet, brings his message of justice, judgment, and repentance in the language of creation. As the Creator, the Lord is sovereign over the nations. As the Creator, the "Lord roars from Zion." God's judgment makes the pastures "wither" and Carmel a desert (Amos 1:2).

The lack of rain, the failure of crops, and bad weather, Amos states, are not an accident. Rather, God is in the mix. Creation has become God's instrument of judgment. The sin of humanity is mirrored in the health of the world. Injustice against the poor has drastic repercussions in the nonhuman realm. Amos finds the scrupulous "church attendance" of his day sickening. It did not translate into loving one's neighbor. "Hear this," Amos heralds, "You trample on the needy and bring to ruin the poor of the land" (Amos 8:4, 10; cf. 4:13).

Israel and land are bound together in judgment and in hope. Expelled from the land in exile, Israel dies. The Creator, however, promises to purify the people. On that day, a resurrection happens. David's house is restored. A restored people mirrored a restored land. Eden returns, Amos declares:

> "The days are coming," declares the Lord,
> "when the reaper will be overtaken by the plowman
> and the planter by the one treading grapes.
> New wine will drip from the mountains
> and flow from all the hills,

and I will bring my people Israel back from exile."
(Amos 9:13–14a NIV)

Amos begins with the withering of the land from Yahweh's judgment but ends on the promise made to Noah and creation: God's people and God's world will be resurrected to Edenic glory.

God's Covenant with the Animals

The life of Hosea is a painful parable on the history of Israel with God. Since the beginning, they had been a people of questionable loyalty, though Yahweh had continually extended mercy. Hosea describes the pitiful situation into which Israel had descended. Adultery covers the land. As a child, Israel did not recognize the care of Yahweh (Hos. 11:1–9). As an adult, Israel fails to seek God. Israel has no real "knowledge" of the Lord. Consequently, God lays a charge against them:

> *Hear the word of the LORD, O people of Israel;*
> *for the LORD has an indictment against the inhabitants of the land.*
> *There is no faithfulness or loyalty*
> *and no knowledge of God in the land. (Hos. 4:1 NRSV)*

The divine imagers have failed miserably to reflect the fundamental character of God. God is faithful—a relationship characterized by *hesed* (God's steadfast love). But Israel's behavior negates her claim to know Yahweh. While Amos notes how zealous Israel was for "church attendance," Hosea baldly states, "There is no knowledge of God in the land." Lack of intimacy with Yahweh reveals itself in fractured human relationships and the vandalism of creation. The Promised Land has reverted to the preflood world. Violence is the law of the land: "Swearing, lying, murder, stealing and adultery break out." The Lord summarizes, "Bloodshed follows bloodshed" (Hos. 4:2). Surprisingly, God declares:

Therefore the land mourns,
and all who live in it languish;
together with the wild animals
and the birds of the air,
even the fish of the sea are perishing. (Hos. 4:3 NRSV)

The text does not say the land is suffering because of judgment. Rather, the land is dying because of human sin. God's own creation is at stake in Israel's sin. Israel is dying, and she is taking the world with her! The suffering of the land testifies to the unfaithfulness of Israel.

The land itself is diseased. The three-fold classification—animals, birds, and fish—is the same as in Psalm 8:7–8, which celebrates the dignity of humanity as the vice-regent of the Creator. God gave humanity "dominion" over these animals. This dominion can only be exercised where the values of faithfulness and *hesed* are applied to the created order by humanity. These royal priests failed, and the anemic, withering, and dying land cries out to the Lord as did the blood-stained ground in Genesis (Gen. 4:11).

The lack of intimacy with Yahweh results in terrible suffering. The most sacred relationships are marred. Widows are neglected. Aliens are exploited. Greed is sanctified. Failure to know God results in a wounded world. Hosea, like other prophets, gives voice to the lamentation of the earth. In nine passages, the Hebrew Bible pictures the land groaning under the weight of sin, longing for redemption (Amos 1:2; Hosea 4:1–4; Jer. 4:23–28; 12:7–13; 23:9–12; Isa. 24:1–24; 33:7–9; Joel 1:5–20).

Many modern ecological disasters illustrate how the earth groans under the weight of human sin. The Aral Sea was the fourth-largest lake on earth in 1960s. Now 90 percent of the lake is gone and replaced with hundreds of square miles of salted sand. What is left is heavily polluted, and the once-important fishery is decimated as well. The resultant economic ruin and the loss of animal habitats have devastated the region. Human abuse has led, as in the days of Israel's prophets, to suffering in both human and nonhuman realms. The earth longs for redemption.

Though the ground suffers under the curse of sin, God has also covenanted with it. God does not accept the status quo. Yahweh is faithful in the face of unfaithfulness. God's commitment to creation becomes Israel's seedbed for hope. God will renew the land and thus resurrect Israel herself.

Hosea 2:14–19 expresses Yahweh's incredible grace. Though entombed in exile, Yahweh will renew covenantal vows with the formerly faithless people. With tender words, the Lord courts and allures Israel. So radical is this renewed relationship, Yahweh exclaims, "You will call me, 'My husband'" (Hos. 2:16). The depth of intimacy the Lord seeks with resurrected Israel is astounding.

God takes the initiative by removing obstacles to a genuine relationship. Therefore, the idols of the land are removed. God's renewed marriage with Israel includes a covenant with the animals:

> I will make for you a covenant with the wild animals, the birds of the air, and the creeping things of the ground; and I will abolish the bow, the sword, and war from the land; and I will make you lie down in safety. And I will take you for my wife in righteousness and in justice, in steadfast love and mercy. I will take you for my wife in faithfulness, and you shall know the LORD. (Hos. 2:18–20 NRSV)

The ground for renewing the broken Sinaitic covenant is God's promise to creation after the flood. This covenant with the animals puts a check on creation's suffering. War, a graphic symbol of human brokenness, is removed from God's land. The bow and the sword, the principle weaponry of the day, can no longer shed blood in the land. As in Isaiah 11:1–9, the establishment of justice brings peace and security as well as a new relationship with animals, which mirror restored human relationships. Without the symbols of humanity's false security, Israel basks in God's own *shalom*. The Lord's own character fills the land because, at long last, the people of God "know the LORD."

The land's laments in Hosea 4:1–3—occasioned by human violence and creation's demise—become the focus of redemption. The redemption of the land is parallel to the redemption of Israel as well as the ground of hope for her redemption. Disruption of the covenant by human sin leads to the destruction of God's creatures, and the land suffers. Yahweh's renewal of the covenant restores an Edenic *shalom* so the land again flows with milk and honey.

Eden Resurrected

The prophet Joel offers us the most comprehensive picture of how sin, lamentation, repentance, and renewal are intertwined. The book of Joel is a communal lament with a divine response. It leads God's people through a liturgical procession.

Joel calls the "inhabitants of the land," the "drunkards," and "priests" (Joel 1:2; 5; 13) to weep, wail, mourn, and cry out. A locust plague, perhaps symbolic of some army, has scorched Palestine. In Joel 1:6–7, as in Jeremiah 8–9, God laments. The army has invaded,

My land . . .
My vines . . .
My fig trees . . .

The ferocity of the devastation leads to a wider participation in lament: "The fields are devastated, the land mourns" (Joel 1:10).

There is nothing left in the land following the invasion. The wine is gone. The crops have disappeared. Things are so bad, brides dress in sackcloth instead of white (Joel 1:8).

What can be done? Joel calls for a solemn assembly in the temple of "all the inhabitants of the land" (Joel 1:15–20). Just as in Hosea 4:1–3, this includes nonhuman participants: "How the animals groan! The herds of cattle wander about because there is no pasture for them" (Joel 1:18). "Even the wild animals cry to you because the watercourses are dried up" (Joel 1:20). They groan like oppressed slaves in Egypt (Ex. 2:23). Lament appeals to God for deliverance. Joel 1 leads God's people and God's creation to their Savior.

Joel 2 reveals the problem. Gathered in solemn assembly, human sin is exposed as the reason for the devastating day of the Lord. Solomon, at the dedication of the temple, warned how locusts were among God's tools to bring about repentance. In repentance, "God will forgive their sin and heal their land" (2 Chron. 6:28; 7:13–14). The locusts, whether Assyrian, Babylonian, or Roman, are representatives of the Creator, the commander in chief. Once again, creation suffers with humanity because of human hubris. The Promised Land is a virtual Garden of Eden raped by sin:

> *Fire devours in front of them,*
> *and behind them a flame burns.*
> *Before them the land is like the garden of Eden,*
> *but after them a desolate wilderness,*
> *and nothing escapes them. (Joel 2:3 NRSV)*

The judgment of God upon Israel reverses creation itself. What was good, beautiful, and full of life has now retreated into a useless void (Gen. 1:2; cf. Jer. 4:23).

Nevertheless, "even now," Yahweh is ready to redeem and heal. God stops the army at the doorstep and offers yet another opportunity for repentance: "Even now," if God's people join in genuine lament, hope remains. The prophet, quoting the "God Creed" (Ex. 34:6–7), declares God "gracious and merciful, slow to anger and abounding in steadfast love, and relents from punishing" (Joel 2:13). In the light of such a gracious proclamation, another solemn assembly is summoned. The people gather before the Lord and the priests stand before the altar to weep in prayer: "Spare your people, O Lord" (Joel 2:17).

God's response to the priestly prayer (Joel 2:18–27) is breathtaking. In fact, this gathering is the hinge of the book (Joel 2:15–17). We move from death to resurrection. Though the army of locusts belonged to God, there was no joy in it (cf. Lam. 3:31–33). The land was "collateral" damage in Yahweh's judgment upon sin: "Then the Lord became jealous for his land, and had pity on his people" (Joel 2:18).

The jealousy of God for the land is akin to his jealousy for Israel. Indeed, they cannot be separated. God has compassion on all creation. Remembering the covenant with creation given after the flood and renewed by Hosea, Yahweh simply refused to extend the damage further. Instead of punishment, God announces three targets of grace:

> *Do not fear, O soil; be glad and rejoice,*
> *for the Lord has done great things!*
> *Do not fear, you animals of the field . . .*
> *O Children of Zion, be glad and*
> *rejoice in the Lord your God. (Joel 2:21–23 NRSV)*

Soil. Animals. People. Bound together in sin. Bound together in redemption. God pours out healing grace. As creation joined humanity in lamentation, so now—as in the psalms—creation joins humanity in praise for the restoration of Eden. So astounding is Yahweh's grace, God seemingly apologizes for the damage done: "I will repay you for the years that the swarming locusts have eaten" (Joel 2:25). What was lost because of sin is restored beyond measure.

As amazing as God's healing grace is to the land, the animals, and the people, this only points to the greatest grace—communion with God. The redemption of creation serves the purpose of God from the beginning: to mediate fellowship with God. After the miracle of salvation, Joel declares, "You shall know that I am in the midst of Israel, and that I, the LORD, am your God" (Joel 2:27). Humanity, expelled from the divine presence, enjoys the redeemed "community of the world" as the Lord comes to dwell within creation again.

Concomitant with the renewal of creation is the pouring out of the Spirit. As the Spirit brought life in the beginning, so now the Spirit restores creation. The inhabitants of the world become the community of the Spirit:

> I will pour out my Spirit on all flesh;
> your sons and your daughters shall prophesy,
> your old men shall dream dreams,
> and your young men shall see visions.
> Even on the male and female slaves,
> in those days, I will pour out my Spirit. (Joel 2:28–29 NRSV)

Restored Eden is radically different from the social structures of the fractured world. Hierarchy, patriarchy, and social position lose their significance in God's new creation. Resurrection is not just a renewed relationship with God but a redefinition of human society itself. The women called by God within Israel in unusual circumstances—Miriam, Deborah, Huldah—are now ordinary.

God's church is a new creation within the old. Peter quotes Joel's text on Pentecost to identify the dawning of the new age (Acts 2:17–18). Less well known is how significant Joel 2 is for Paul. Paul's appeal to baptism as our incorporation into the Abrahamic covenant in which all people shall be blessed echoes Joel's promise:

Galatians 3:26–28	Joel 2:28–29
Jew/Greek	All flesh
Male/female	Sons/daughters
Free/slave	Free/slave

Renewed Israel is the place where the old power structures are removed. Yet we still wait for the final consummation of Eden's return.

CONCLUSION

The story of Israel and the land is the story of humanity and the world. Israel and the land are redeemed for the sake of the world. Therefore, the resurrection of Israel, the land, and the restoration of communion with God point to God's ultimate fulfillment of the purpose of creation in the eschaton. Dreams of Eden are visions of life as it was intended in creation, where we inhabit a world dominated by God's righteousness, *hesed*, and *shalom*. The prophets, especially Joel, anticipate the supreme blessing of new creation of Revelation 21–22: "The LORD dwells in Zion" surrounded by descriptions of Edenic beauty.

BULLET POINTS

- The prophets of Israel stressed the symbiotic relationship between human and nonhuman creation.
- Human sin has drastic results in the cosmic sphere.
- Humans are bound to the world in corruption just as they are in redemption.

QUESTIONS

1. What is the significance of the Noahic covenant in biblical faith? What does it say about God, humanity, and creation?

2. What contemporary examples illustrate how human corruption causes the land to mourn?

3. How would care for creation give the church a prophetic witness? Why is the church often hesitant to give such a witness?

CHAPTER SIX

The Christ Event, Creation, and New Creation

Immortality, in the sacred writings, is never applied to the spirit of man. It is not the doctrine of Plato which the resurrection of Jesus proposes. It is the immortality of the body of which his resurrection is a proof and pledge. This was never developed till he became the first born from the dead, and in a human body entered the heavens. Jesus was not a spirit when he returned to God. He is not made the Head of the New Creation as a Spirit but as the Son of Man. Our nature in his person is glorified; and when he appears to our salvation, we shall be made like him: we shall then see him as he is. This is the Christian hope.

—Alexander Campbell[1]

The "Christ Event" is a shorthand way of saying "the incarnation, ministry, death, resurrection, ascension, and enthronement of Jesus the Messiah." This is the gospel, the good news. God reconciled the world, healed its brokenness, and redeemed it through Christ. Jesus the Messiah is the paramount act of God, which reorders the cosmos so that everything in heaven and earth is once again placed under God's sovereignty (Eph. 1:9–10).

All God's promises are "yes" in Jesus the Messiah (2 Cor. 1:20) and, consequently, all the hopes for humanity and God's good creation are centered in Jesus who redeems all creation as God reconciles "all things, whether on earth or heaven," through him (Col. 1:20). The "Christ Event," then, is what God has done in Jesus the Messiah to set the world right and liberate it from its lingering bondage.

Incarnation: Union of God and Humanity

If humanity had never sinned, would God have still become "flesh"?

More happened in the incarnation than simply preparing a perfect human for a sacrificial offering. Because God's purpose from the beginning was communion with humanity—to draw them into the love the Father and the Son share (John 17:20–26)—the incarnation becomes the ultimate means by which God fully unites with, empathizes with, and loves humanity. God becomes human in order to fully "know" humanity.

When the Word became "flesh" and shared the materiality of the earth, the Word dwelt (tabernacled) with humanity. The enfleshed God joined humanity by dwelling as flesh upon a material earth. Just as God in the beginning dwelt with humanity on the earth in the Garden and then later dwelt with Israel in the tabernacle and temple, so through incarnation God dwelt with humanity in the life and ministry of Jesus. God joined humanity in God's "resting place," which is creation. Wondrously, God not only joined us here but also became part of creation itself in order to fully dwell with us in intimate communion.

The progression in John 1:1–18 is important:

The Word is God from the beginning.
The Word brings light into darkness.

The Word becomes flesh.

The Word dwells among us.

Humanity sees the "glory" of God.

Just as we see the "glory of God" through the heavens (Ps. 19:1), so we also see the "glory" of God through the enfleshed Word. The flesh is neither evil nor peripheral. It is creation, and creation is good and holy. Through the incarnation, the flesh has become the resting place of the divine, just as—in the beginning—creation itself was a divine resting place (Isa. 66:1–2) and will be again in the new heaven and new earth (Rev. 21:1–4).

Consequently, the incarnation also has significance for creation. The Gospel of John begins with creation ("in the beginning") and recognizes how the incarnation introduced light into the darkness, just as on the first day of creation. However, the first day did not eliminate darkness, and only the light was called "good"—not the darkness, which is part of the primordial chaos. The incarnation completes creation and defeats the darkness—both what has been introduced since creation and what was part of the original elements in Genesis 1:2. Jesus, as incarnate God, dispels the darkness through suffering and death, which inaugurates new creation through resurrection. God personally acts through incarnation to overcome the darkness in the present world, but darkness will not be part of the new heaven and new earth. There will be no night there (Rev. 21:25).

The incarnation is the ultimate divine commentary on the goodness of creation, the seal of God's pronouncement, "It was very good" (Gen. 1:31). Whatever darkness may have existed within creation and whatever humanity added to that darkness, the incarnation sanctified creation and announced its goodness, since God entered creation and became flesh, a human creature.

"The Word became flesh" (John 1:14). This means more than God became human. "Flesh" is the Hebraic way of speaking about creation. In the flood story, "all flesh" is destroyed, and the post-flood covenant is made with "all flesh," including the animals (Gen. 9:8–11). God gives life to "all flesh" (Job 34:14–15), God sustains "all flesh" (Ps. 136:25), and "all flesh" praises God (Ps. 145:21). God assumes "flesh"—that is, materiality. The Word becomes part of creation itself and communes with nature. The one through whom "all things" (John 1:3; the whole universe) were brought into being unites with "all things" by becoming "flesh" (a material reality).

God, then, becomes part of creation itself. God unites with creation, and this union is neither temporary nor a throwaway add-on. When the Word became human, the Word became forever human (our eternal brother in the resurrection) and thus forever part of creation.

Creation is not only good; it is now eternal because God has united himself with it. In his incarnation, Jesus fully participates in creation and guarantees not only the goodness of creation but its liberation from its bondage in darkness. Through his resurrection, Jesus establishes a new fate for creation—it will be an eternal, never-ending reality. The fate of creation is now eternally bound to the resurrected Jesus.

Ministry in Galilee

The ministry of Jesus in Galilee is a proleptic experience of God's future reclamation of the whole earth.

Matthew frames his gospel against the backdrop of Isaiah 7–12, where the prophet addresses Ahaz, the king of Judah. Fearful of Israel and Syria, Ahaz allies with Assyria rather than trusting the Lord. Assyria overruns Israel. Isaiah sees a future when "darkness" descends upon the "Galilee of the nations" in "the land of Zebulun and the land of Naphtali" (Isa. 9:1).

However, Isaiah promises a future day when God will lift the oppression, defeat the enemy, and enlarge the nation (Isa. 9:3–5). God will secure this victory through the birth of a child, Immanuel—"God with us" (Isa. 7:14; 8:8–10; 9:6; cf. Matt. 1:23). This child, as Matthew applies Isaiah, is the Messiah, Jesus of Nazareth. He is the prince of peace whose dominion is vast and peaceful. Sitting on the throne of David, he establishes righteousness forever (Isa. 9:6–7). This is the root of Jesse upon whom the Spirit of God rests, and the Messiah distributes justice and equity to the "poor" and the "meek of the earth" (Isa. 11:1–5). On that day, the nations will seek the Messiah, *shalom* will return to the earth (lambs and leopards, cows and lions, and children and snakes will live together as in Eden), and the "knowledge of the LORD" will fill the earth (Isa. 11:6–10).

When Jesus began his ministry in Galilee, the fulfillment of Isaiah's prophecy also began (Matt. 4:12–17). Jesus "left Nazareth and made his home"—literally, came to dwell—in the land of "Zebulun and Naphtali." In that moment, in the language of Isaiah,

> *The people walking in darkness*
> *have seen a great light,*
> *and for those living in the land of deep darkness*
> *a light has dawned. (Isa. 9:2 NIV)*

The language echoes creation—light and darkness. Jesus enters the darkness (Galilee of the Gentiles) as God's light and fills it with divine glory. God comes to dwell in Galilee as Jesus makes his home in Capernaum. Matthew uses the same word in 4:13 that is used in 23:21, which describes how God dwells in the temple. Just as

God dwells in the temple, so Jesus dwells in Galilee. Indeed, Jesus believes God is present in him in a way that is greater than God's presence in the temple (cf. Matt. 12:6). Jesus is the new temple who dwells with humanity in the flesh!

The ministry of Jesus is the beginning of God's creation reclamation project. It begins in northern Israel where Assyria first annexed and exiled God's people to other lands. It continues when Jesus enters Jerusalem, and it spreads throughout the whole earth through God's restored Israel, including the church.

Just as Israel crossed the sea, trekked through the wilderness, and entered the land of promise, so Jesus was baptized, tried in the wilderness, and entered the land of promise to inaugurate God's retrieval of the earth as God's dwelling place. Just as Israel dwelt in the land and God "rested" with them in the temple, so Jesus comes to dwell in the land and, as God's new temple (one "greater than the Temple is here" [Matt. 12:6]), God rests with Israel in the land.

God rested in the land through the ministry of Jesus in order to reclaim the land for God's kingdom. Indeed, Jesus articulates this goal in one of his beatitudes: "Blessed are the meek for they shall inherit the earth" (Matt. 5:5 KJV).

Death of Jesus as Full Participation in Old Creation

Whatever the death of Jesus means for salvation—many metaphors and theories describe it—it at least involves the incarnate one's full participation in the human condition. Through incarnation, ministry, and now death, the Son fully participates in creation, including its brokenness. Hostile powers humiliated him and killed him. Through death, Jesus experienced creation's bondage. Death, which enslaves both humanity and the whole of creation, captured Jesus, and Jesus descended into Hades (the realm of the dead, Acts 2:31).

When God became flesh, God did not become transfigured flesh or immortal flesh. Rather, through becoming flesh, God was subjected to the all the frailties, bondage, and weaknesses of the present, broken creation. The "old creation" is what now exists. Death reigns. Suffering prevails. The flesh deteriorates. This is the old world, which groans and yearns for liberation and redemption.

Jesus participated in the "old creation." He thirsted and hungered, like other humans and animals exiled from Eden. He suffered and he died. His flesh lost its breath and was entombed. Jesus did not simply skirt the edges of the "old creation." On the contrary, he was fully immersed in it, even lamenting on the cross about how God had abandoned him to the grave (Mark 15:34; Ps. 22:1; 104:29).

Becoming flesh within this "old creation," God suffered and died. As a result, God became fully empathetic with humanity. God understands the human condition in more than a cognitive sense. God has now experienced hunger, thirst, temptation, and death. God knows brokenness through God's own experience of the "old creation" through Jesus.

In Jesus, God dwelt in an enslaved creation, bound over to death—a mortal creature, fully participating in the Adamic, old creation. Rather than abandoning creation to its bondage, God came to liberate it and renew it.

Resurrection as Beginning of New Creation

New creation began with the Christ Event—the incarnation, ministry, death, resurrection, and ascension of Jesus the Messiah.

In one sense, Christology is eschatology. The resurrection birthed a new humanity belonging to the new heaven and new earth; Jesus is the firstborn from the dead (Rev. 1:5; Col. 1:18). But we might also think about the death of Jesus as eschatological as well. His death was, in some sense, the experience of a second death, or an eschatological death, for our sakes. Jesus experienced death for us and transformed death through the resurrection. Also, the ministry of Jesus proclaimed the good news of the kingdom, and his kingdom works proclaimed creation's future. That future—diseases healed, demons expelled, death reversed—broke into the present through the ministry of Jesus. Jesus's healing ministry reversed creation's curse as it heralded the coming kingdom. Incarnation is eschatological as the ultimate union of God and humanity.

Death is the epitome of the broken world; it is the last enemy (1 Cor. 15:26). This parasitic enemy terrorizes all creation, fostering doubt and fear. God's hope is not a disembodied, immortal soul living in heaven but an immortal human being (body and soul) living upon the new earth, the home of the righteous (2 Peter 3:13).

The resurrection of Jesus inaugurates new creation. The old, Adamic humanity, with its mortal body enslaved to death and corruption, is redeemed through a birth from the dead. The resurrection of Jesus is no resuscitation. Rather, the Adamic body is transformed into a new body appropriate for the new heaven and new earth. Jesus is new humanity, including a renewed body—the first to emerge from Hades prepared for new creation.

Jesus, as the resurrected new human, is the first fruits of the harvest, which is the redeemed people of God, new humanity (1 Cor. 15:20–23). The first fruits were the initial part of the annual crops offered to God in acknowledgement of God's blessing. This grateful offering trusted that God would bring the rest of the harvest to fruition.

The resurrection of Jesus and the resurrection of believers are one; they belong to the same harvest and continuum. They are a single, though two-stage, event in redemptive history. The resurrection of Jesus is proleptic, as it initiates new creation within the old creation. The resurrection of Jesus, though a historic reality, belongs to the future and assures creation's future. The resurrection of Jesus, then, is the pledge of a future harvest, a preview of coming attractions. It is God's answer to creation's lament.

Jesus is first—the firstborn from the dead. But he is more—he is the pattern. We will bear the image of the heavenly human, the second Adam, just as we now bear the image of the first Adam. Christ is the new humanity. We will participate in his new humanity and our bodies will be like his (1 Cor. 15:49; Phil. 3:21).

Resurrected new humanity, patterned after and grounded in the resurrection of Jesus, is the Christian hope. The contrast between our present Adamic existence within this old creation and our future Christic existence in the new creation is the contrast between mortal and immortal, dishonor and glory, weakness and power, and "natural" and "spiritual" (1 Cor. 15:42–44).

The "natural" (literally, "soulish") body is a material substance animated and nourished by "flesh and blood"—our present Adamic existence. The "spiritual" body is a material substance animated by heavenly resources, as the Holy Spirit sustains new humanity. New humanity, in both body and spirit, lives by the power of the Spirit of God—this is the meaning of "Spiritual." Conformed to the image of Christ's own resurrected body, resurrected humanity will live in new bodies upon the new earth—under new heavens—as part of the new creation in communion with God.

Enthronement of New Humanity

The ascension of the Messiah to the Davidic throne after the resurrection is the climactic eschatological event. Raised from the dead and exalted as the Son of Man, Christ ascended to the right hand of the Father as King of Kings (Eph. 1:19). From there, he pours out the Spirit upon the people of God, rules over creation as he dispels chaos and death, and intercedes for his people.

Most significantly, the resurrected Messiah, as new the human, unites heaven and earth. His glorious humanity (immortal body and soul) lives in the presence of God, and one day he will live in the new Jerusalem upon a new earth. The messianic reign is the reign of new humanity preparing a new Jerusalem for a new heaven and earth.

Seated at the right hand of God, his reign breaks into the "old creation" to reverse the curse, just as he did in his ministry. The people of God continue that ministry as servants of the king. And the king will reign over this "old creation" until every enemy is put under his feet, and the last enemy is death (1 Cor. 15:26). Then the enthroned king will descend to the new earth with his resurrected saints and there reign with them forever. When humanity is fully restored in the image of Jesus, their elder brother, humanity will again serve as royal priests within God's new creation where death no longer enslaves God's good creation (1 Thess. 4:16; 1 Cor. 15:26; Rev. 5:10; 11:15; 21:1–4; 22:5)

CONCLUSION

God became flesh and united creation to God's own self. God dwelt within creation as a creature, a human being. God suffered, groaned, and died under the bondage afflicting creation—God suffered with creation. God liberated creation from death through the resurrection of Jesus. God, as Jesus the Messiah, is presently enthroned at the right hand of the Father as the foundation and beginning of new creation itself and one day will return to a renewed earth to reign forever with resurrected humanity.

BULLET POINTS

- God completes the story of creation by becoming part of creation itself through the incarnation of the Word as Jesus the Messiah.
- God began the reclamation of the earth for the kingdom of God through the ministry of Jesus.
- Though God experienced the brokenness of creation through the death of Jesus, and God inaugurated new creation in the resurrection and enthronement of Jesus the Messiah.

QUESTIONS

1. What significance do you attach to *flesh* and *creation* when you remember God became flesh? What is the meaning of the incarnation in relation to creation?

2. Why is it important in your own journey that God shares your experience of creation's brokenness through Jesus?

3. If new creation has already begun, how do you experience this in your own life?

CHAPTER SEVEN

God's *Shofar*

The Jubilee Mission of Jesus

JUBILEE! Let the slave and captive go free
JUBILEE! Save the land and return it to me
JUBILEE! Let the people stand in their dignity
In the year of God's Jubilee.

—Jim Strathdee[1]

Throughout Scripture, the people placed within God's world, like leaven in the lump, spread death rather than life. Time and again God anointed prophets to renew Israel in her mission. The more Yahweh pursued, the more they squandered the covenant of love (Hos. 11:1–4). Israel's sin led not only to her death in exile but also to the pollution of God's land. The sin against the land was so oppressive, God sent Israel into exile to grant the land Sabbath rest, which it had never enjoyed (2 Chron. 36:21).

The weekly Sabbath, the Sabbath year, and Jubilee are woven into each other like the threads of a rope. These cords bring together two key biblical themes—creation and redemption. Each Sabbath day, Israel celebrated creation of the world as it came from God's hand as well as its redemption from Egyptian slavery (Ex. 20:10–11;

Deut. 5:15). This weekly rhythm established a tone of gratitude, which remembers the gift of creation and Israel's liberation from Egypt.

Sabbath remembers creation and liberation, and Jubilee frees creation and captives in the present. This spiritual wisdom moves the Sabbath from weekly remembrance to living. Every seven years, grace is proclaimed, granting rest to the poor and the land (Deut. 15). Every fifty years, a Sabbath of Sabbaths is proclaimed on the Day of Atonement. After the High Priest confesses the brokenness of the world over the scapegoat and the blood is brought into the Holy of Holies, the priest emerges from the sanctuary and God's *shofar* is blown:

> *You shall have the trumpet sounded loud throughout the land . . .*
> *You shall hallow the fiftieth year . . .*
> *You shall proclaim liberty throughout the land to all its*
> *inhabitants . . .*
> *It shall be a jubilee for you . . .*
> *You shall return, every one of you, to your property and every*
> *one of you to your people . . .*
> *It is a jubilee; it shall be holy to you. (Lev. 25 NRSV)*

The weekly Sabbath, the Sabbath year, and Jubilee are about people and land, creation and redemption. They remember the way the world was in the beginning and project what the world will be in the future, which serves as a pattern for the present. When God's *shofar* is blown, the world returns to its glorious condition on the first Sabbath of creation. Jubilee envisions an Eden absent of oppression, suffering, sin, and death. Jubilee proclaims the healing of the world, God's *shalom*.

God's people failed. Creation lamented. Prophets dreamed. God acted.

God's Nazareth Manifesto

Luke identifies a seismic shift in the story of God with the incarnation of Jesus. The Spirit who hovered over the water of creation—bringing life to the world and birthing Adam—overshadowed Mary in the virginal conception of Jesus. As God surrounded Adam with the animals, so the manger and the angelic army's announcement to shepherds pointed to creation's participation in the drama of salvation. The Warrior of God, Gabriel, announced God's intent to reclaim creation by reversing the curse and restoring *shalom*.

When Jesus entered his hometown synagogue at the beginning of his ministry, it was not like other occasions. The attendant handed Jesus the Isaiah scroll. Opening to the correct column near the end, Jesus read:

> *The Spirit of the Lord is upon me,*
> *because he has anointed me*
> *to bring good news to the poor.*
> *He has sent me to proclaim release to captives*
> *and recovery of sight to the blind,*
> *to let the oppressed go free,*
> *to proclaim the year of the Lord's favor. (Luke 4:18–19; cf.*
> *Isa. 61:1–2 NRSV)*

This cherished text from Isaiah 61 proclaims the Year of Jubilee. Indicative of its significance, it was central to the messianic dreams of devout Jews at Qumran, where Melchizedek was sent by God to inaugurate God's new age by proclaiming freedom from sin and debt.[2] Jesus's interpretation of the passage was deliberate and explosive: "Today this scripture has been fulfilled in your hearing" (Luke 4:22). But Jesus does not simply read Isaiah 61. He adds a line from another great Sabbath text, Isaiah 58. The addition of

Isaiah 58:6 to 61:1–2 only intensifies the Nazareth Manifesto "to let the oppressed go free."

Jesus was baptized in the Spirit who had brought him into the world. That Spirit, who hovered over the chaotic waters in Genesis 1, empowered him for his anointed mission as God's Messiah—the *shofar* of God's Jubilee. He succeeded in God's mission where Adam and Israel failed. Jesus's whole life became an atoning Jubilee for the sin of humanity and the suffering of creation. If Jubilee is here, then so is Yom Kippur, the Day of Atonement.

Jubilee, Four Rich Men, and Salvation

Luke does not "spiritualize" the Jubilee mission of Jesus. Jesus sets free the poor, the captive, the blind, and the oppressed. His mission is as holistic as Sabbath and Jubilee. Jesus is humanity's most subversive revolutionary. The Nazareth Manifesto does not come by force of arms; it comes through healing creation. When John the Baptizer, languishing in prison, questioned Jesus's methods, the Lord's reply was that the *shofar* has blown: "Go and tell John what you have seen and heard: the blind receive their sight, the lame walk, the lepers are cleansed, the deaf hear, the dead are raised, the poor have the good news brought to them" (Luke 7:22). The good news Jesus preached had concrete "physical" dimensions. Jubilee salvation did not evaporate into Platonic dualism.

The Jubilary age, which Jesus heralded, creates a culture *within* God's hurting world. Composed of liberated people, they embrace Jubilee as a matter of course. That culture calls for inclusivity where even the poor are called to love their enemies. The social dimension of God's Nazareth Manifesto becomes clear in the beatitudes:

> *Blessed are you who are poor,*
> *for yours is the kingdom of God.*

Blessed are you who are hungry now,
for you will be filled.
Blessed are you who weep now,
for you will laugh . . . *(Luke 6:20–21; emphasis ours)*

Jesus confronts those on the opposite side of the social spectrum:

But woe to you who are rich,
for you have received your consolation.
Woe to you who are full now,
for you will be hungry.
Woe to you who are laughing now,
for you will mourn and weep spectrum. (Luke 6:24–25;
emphasis ours)

When the zealots captured the temple at the beginning of the Jewish Revolt in the first century, they burned the records of debt. Jesus, however, executes God's Jubilee through means other than violence. Debt, ubiquitous in Palestine, referred to both economic debt and spiritual alienation. Alienation from God manifests itself in the vandalism of all God's creation.

The meaning of Jubilee becomes clear in Luke's four stories of rich men. Two are unique to his gospel. Each person is confronted with the demand of Jubilee.

First, when asked to divide an inheritance, Jesus told a parable about a rich fool who builds bigger barns for the bounty he reaped from the earth. The builder intended to hoard, consume, and live in comfort. But the God of Jubilee declared, "You fool! This very night your life will be demanded of you" (Luke 12:13–21).

In a second story, only found in Luke, we find a rich man contrasted with Lazarus, who is called a *ptochos* (a poor person; Luke 16:20), a word found in both Jesus's beatitude and the Nazareth

Manifesto. The parable highlights a self-absorbed society where those in poverty are completely hidden in plain view of the wealthy. As with the rich fool, this man trades places with Lazarus. He is in torment and Lazarus rests in paradise.

A third rich person came to Jesus. He had dedicated his life to the commandments of God but thought he could love God without loving his neighbor. He was faithful in all except Jubilee: "There is one thing still lacking. Sell all that you own and distribute the money to the poor" (Luke 18:22). But the "rich ruler" loved his money more than his poor neighbors and, therefore, more than God.

The fourth story is unique to Luke's Gospel. Zacchaeus is not only rich but a chief tax collector and "a sinner" (Luke 19:7). God's *shofar* graciously initiated a relationship by offering to stay at his house. Zacchaeus responded by doing what the other three were unwilling to do—he embraced Jubilee. He repented of the misuse of money, gave away half of his wealth, and repaid those he defrauded four times the amount he swindled. Jesus announced, "Today *salvation* has come to this house," and then added, "The Son of Man came to seek and *save* what was lost" (Luke 19:9–10; emphasis ours).

These four stories in Luke highlight the concrete social dimension of salvation. The healing of the vertical relationship with God is manifested in healing—in concrete terms—fractured human relationships. When Jubilee happens, so does the Day of Atonement.

Jubilee Tables

Meals are a major theme in Luke, but it is not about eating. Viewing Jesus's meals through the lens of segregation in the time of Jim Crow laws in the United States, we begin to understand the significance of Jesus's controversial eating habits. Meals play an important social function in reinforcing the stratification of society.

Just as eating at the same counter would imply equality between white and black, sitting at a table in another's home declares kinship. For Jesus, meals took Jubilee out of the rarified air of theory and placed it directly into the grit of life. If Jubilee proclaims the healing of God's world, then there is no better place to bear witness than at a meal. Jesus eats with "tax collectors and sinners" (Luke 5:27–32; 7:33–35; 15:1–2; 19:1–10). A meal with Simon becomes an occasion for Jubilee action. Allowing a woman, a sinner, to touch him scandalized Simon. Then Jesus told a story about two people in debt—one in a small amount and another in a large amount. Neither was able to repay the debt. The creditor graciously released (forgave) both debts (Luke 7:41–42). Simon did not miss the import of the parable. Jesus welcomed this woman: "Your sins are forgiven" (Luke 7:48). The captive was set free.

Luke highlights the radical table ministry of Jesus in the Parable of the Great Jubilee Banquet (Luke 14:15–24). The table mirrors kingdom theology. Whom we invite and where we sit identifies the narrative in which we live. For Jesus, the kingdom subverts the broken and suffering world. The guest list is composed of those who cannot reciprocate. Challenging our standard association with those of the same class and status, Jesus reverses the social privilege of the powerful, and they are excluded from the banquet. Jesus says, "Go out at once into the streets and lanes of the town and bring in the poor, the crippled, the blind and the lame" (Luke 14:21). Meals in the kingdom are for those normally excluded from the fractured world's guest list. At the table, the divisions of the world are reimagined into a new narrative—a world where there is no Jew or Greek, male or female, slave or freeman.

Meals play a significant role in the ongoing life of God's people. The primary furniture for early Christian assemblies was not a pulpit but a table. At the table, in breaking common bread, the resurrected Lord communes with us. The table not only remembers Jesus and his mission but announces and embodies this new narrative as an alternative community in the world. Luke connects the church's habit of breaking bread in homes with their mutual sharing of possessions (Acts 2:42–47; 4:32–35). The rich abundance of the Creator was not hoarded selfishly in a barn like the rich fool did but graciously made available to all in need. The spirit of Jubilee pervades Christian community when it understands the radical significance of the Lord's Table, which empowers disciples today with the aroma of Christ.

Jubilee Community

The story of Jesus does not end with his crucifixion and resurrection; he is enthroned at the right hand of the Father. On Pentecost, which celebrates the Creator's ownership of the earth's bounty as well as the giving of the covenant at Sinai, the exalted Christ poured out the Holy Spirit, baptizing the one hundred twenty in the Spirit, restoring Israel in fulfillment of Joel's prophecy (Acts 2).

A loud, violent blast, evocative of Mount Sinai, filled the temple, and fire appeared above the waiting disciples. The Spirit, who empowered Jesus for God's mission, clothed the huddled band of believers with power from on high. God began to fulfill his promises made to Abraham, David, and the prophets in new way. The pouring of the Spirit applies the victory of the death and resurrection to the healing of the world. Restored Israel, Luke stresses, embodies Jesus's Jubilee table ministry because, as Joel prophesied, the Holy Spirit renews God's people as a new creation:

> In the last days it will be, God declares,
> that I will pour out my Spirit upon all flesh,

and your sons and your daughters shall prophesy,
and your young men shall see visions,
and your old men shall dream dreams.
Even upon my slaves, both men and women,
in those days I will pour my Spirit;
and they shall prophesy. (Acts 2:17–18 NRSV)

The ministry, death, resurrection, and ascension of Jesus did not birth a religion focused on a private, personal relationship with God. Rather, in keeping the promises to Abraham, it resulted in the renewing of the ancient people of God for the sake of healing the entire world. Salvation created a Jubilee community of reconciliation, which erases the fault lines of humanity. God's people, now the temple of God's Spirit, know nothing of the divisive interests of status, economics, and patriarchy. Restored relationships with each other mirror our restored relationship with God.

The Holy Spirit anointed Jesus to proclaim the new age of liberty and God's favor. Peter, baptized in the same Spirit, also proclaimed that message. Though blood stained their hands from the murder of the "Author of Life" (Acts 3:15), Peter invited them to share in the Age of Jubilee. "Repent, be baptized, therefore, each of you, to have freedom [*aphesin*] from your sins" (Acts 2:38; our translation). Peter's language is the same as the anointed Jesus, to "proclaim freedom [*aphesin*] for the prisoners" (Luke 4:18 NIV). The Greek word *aphesis* peppers the Septuagint's translation of Leviticus 25 (fourteen times) and Deuteronomy 15:1–4 (fifteen times), prominent Sabbath and Jubilee texts. The Spirit created the church as a Jubilee community within God's hurting world.

Baptism into God's renewed Israel results in freedom from guilt and also has actual consequences within creation. Sin is not only alienation from God. Sin antagonizes every dimension of creation. The fruit of baptism is a Jubilee community where there is economic sharing (Acts 2:41–47) and gracious hospitality (Acts 10:47–48; 16:14–15, 28–34). In other words, God's Jubilee creates a new world within the old world as an advertisement for the coming new heaven and new earth.

Missional Creation

Sabbath and Jubilee are intensely creational in focus. Israel celebrated the goodness of the world from the Creator's hand. Even for those without the Torah, creation proclaims the majesty of God. Creation is missional. Twice Paul applied this theology while spreading the good news among Gentile pagans. At Lystra, Paul appealed to creation to establish common humanity with the idolaters. The benevolent Creator has "made the heavens and the earth and the sea and all that is in them." Yahweh is not only the God of Israel. The Creator lovingly provides for all people, even those who do not acknowledge God, and fills their hearts with "joy" (Acts 14:8–20).

Similarly, in Athens—the capital of pagan culture—Paul digs from the robust Jewish doctrine of creation to share the gospel (Acts 17:16–34). Complementing the Greeks on their pious disposition, he crafts a sermon around an altar for "an unknown god" (Acts 17:23). Paul announces the unknown Creator to the nations. Creation, like Jubilee, acknowledges the essential oneness of humanity. Israel's God has shepherded the pagan nations, even setting boundaries for them like Israel. The one true God is not left without witness, even in pagan literature. Quoting Epimenides and Aratus, Paul springboards into Jesus and his resurrection. For Luke, creation points to the lover and healer of the world.

CONCLUSION

Together Luke and Acts emphasize a critical theme: Jesus's ministry in healing, preaching, eating, dying, and pouring out the Spirit announces God's Jubilee has come. God has begun the healing of creation. Jubilee follows atonement. It appropriates the symbolized removal of guilt in the present and ushers in Jubilee, which reminds us how God is healing the whole world. Jubilee is for the lame, blind, and oppressed, and it brings them into a relationship with God by placing them in an ancient but renewed community. Jubilee is God's concrete picture of salvation itself! Thus Jesus created a people who live by and for the sake of forgiveness. Christ's community is at one with God, at one with each other, and at one with creation. Knowing atonement ("at-one-ment"), it pursues a ministry of reconciliation.

BULLET POINTS

- Jubilee is the insertion of grace into history for the healing of creation.
- Jesus is God's Jubilee, restoring creation through his healing ministry and setting captives free.
- The church, empowered by the Spirit, continues God's Jubilee mission by becoming a Jubilee community within creation.

QUESTIONS

1. What is God's Nazareth Manifesto? How is this also the church's manifesto? In what ways do you see this at work in your community?

2. In what ways does the ministry of Jesus participate in the healing of creation? How might this extend through the church as well?

3. How would you define a Jubilee community, and how might the church become that?

CHAPTER EIGHT

The Gospel of Promise

Resurrected Lord, Resurrected People, and the Resurrected World

But—thanks be to God—through Jesus Christ grace came with a mighty hand to meet this great, dark, cursing, onrushing tide of woe and death, to roll it back, to free men from death and the earth from every curse of sin, and to give to it a glory and beauty never dreamed of by Adam and Eve in the midst of their Edenic home. This earth, with its surrounding heaven, is to be made over, and on the fair face of the new earth God himself will dwell with all the sons and daughters of men who have been redeemed through grace . . . through Adam we lost the garden of Eden; through Christ we gain the paradise of God.

—James A. Harding[1]

Paul, Jesus, and all pious Jews in the Second Temple period lived in a "storied" universe. An all-encompassing dramatic story gave life meaning. It was the story of the faithful promise-keeping God and included the promises to Abraham, the promises of the Exodus, the promises to David and Zion, the promises of the Psalms, and the promises of the prophets. This story, poured into hearts and minds of the early church through Scripture and liturgy, is the DNA of renewed Israel's faith. God fulfilled these promises through Jesus the Messiah: "For in him every one of God's promises is a 'Yes'" (2 Cor. 1:20).

The Gospel of Promise

Paul calls these promises "the gospel" and makes them the cornerstone of his inclusion of the Gentiles among the heirs of Abraham. While "the promises were made to Abraham and to his offspring," he writes, "if you belong to Christ, then you are Abraham's offspring according to the promise" (Gal. 3:16, 29). God promised Abraham's family an inheritance of land where God would dwell with them, and through that promise, God intended to bless all nations. Abraham and the land represent the nations and creation. This promise appears throughout the Hebrew Bible:

> I will make you a great nation, and I will bless you, and I will make your name great, so that you will be a blessing, I will bless those who bless you, and the one who curses you I will curse; and in you all the families of the earth shall be blessed . . . Then the Lord appeared to Abram, and said, "To your offspring I will give this land." (Gen. 12:1–3, 7; cf. 17:7–8; 28:13–14, 21)

> I am the LORD, and I will free you from the burdens of the Egyptians and deliver you from slavery to them . . . I will take you as my people and I will be your God . . . I will bring you into the land that I sword to give to Abraham, Isaac, and Jacob. (Ex. 6:6–8)

> But as for you, the LORD took you out of the iron-smelting furnace, out of Egypt, to be the people of his inheritance, as you now are. (Deut. 4:20)

Additionally, the promise is taken up into the Davidic covenant, whose "heritage" is "the ends of the earth" along with the people dwelling on them (Ps. 2:8–9; 22:27–28; 72:8–11). It is also the cornerstone of David's rededication of the tabernacle, the symbol of God's dwelling in the land (1 Chron. 16:15–36).

The fulfilled promise is the goal of salvation, which reveals God's faithfulness. So many either apply the fulfillment of the promise to the modern state of Israel or spiritualize it as equivalent to the church. But Paul, with the sweep of the story behind him, points to something beyond a strip of land between the Jordan and the Mediterranean: "For the promise that he would *inherit the world* did not come to Abraham or to *his descendants* through the law but through the righteousness of faith" (Rom. 4:13; emphasis ours). What is this "world" (cosmos) Abraham and his descendants are to inherit? Before we answer that question, let's listen to a song.

Christ of Creation and Redemption

False teaching, which some call "proto-Gnosticism," troubled believers in Colossae. These disciples lived in fear of spiritual powers and angelic beings that supposedly shared the divine nature in some fashion.

Paul addresses the theological issues underlying this problem by quoting what most believe is an early Christian hymn that applies the story of hope understood through Christ. Verses 15–16 form the first strophe, with a link, or interlude, in verse 17, followed by verses 18–20, which form the second strophe.

The Christ Hymn is breathtaking in its claims. Believers should not worry about the powers, thrones, or angelic beings precisely because everything in the cosmos was created through Christ. Paul wastes no time arguing whether these beings exist. Instead, if they exist, he argues, they were created through Christ. Hear the apostle's melody:

> He is the image of the invisible God, the firstborn of all creation, for in him all things in heaven and on earth were created, things visible and invisible, whether thrones, or dominions or principalities or powers—all things have been created through him and for him. (Col. 1:15–16)

Though Paul thoroughly knows Genesis 1, he astonishingly claims the man from Galilee was Yahweh's instrument of creation. Knowing Christ created those angelic thugs makes them a little less intimidating—they are mere creations. The Messiah is supreme over the powers because he is the instrument of creation.

Paul reframes the Colossian worldview by bringing them a Christ-centered story of creation. Creation is good because Christ Jesus made it so. It is beautiful, powerful, and wonderful because Christ made it like that.

As beautiful as creation is, there is also ugliness. Fear and death symbolize that ugliness. Something went awry in creation. Like most Romans, the Colossians lived in perpetual fear. Creation had rebelled. When God, through Christ, created the cosmos (seen and unseen), those angelic beings were among God's good creatures. While Paul does not explain how or when they became such, they are now enemies of God's people. Consequently, just prior to quoting the Christ Hymn, Paul appropriates Exodus language to talk about God's great "rescue operation" in Jesus: "For he has rescued us from the dominion of darkness" (Col. 1:13). When God rescued Israel, he destroyed the enemy's armies. Likewise, Christ destroys the power of his enemies.

In the next chapter, Paul uses combat imagery to describe Christ's work in the cosmic realm. The enemies of God's people used the *cheirograph* (record) against them but Christ nailed it to the cross (Col. 2:14). Having "disarmed the powers and authorities, he made a public spectacle of them, triumphing over them by the cross" (Col. 2:15). Likely, some thought the cross was evidence of what happens to anyone who dares to oppose the "powers." Paul, however, pulls back the curtain. Far from defeat, the crucifixion was a stunning victory. As Yahweh utterly defeated the "gods of Egypt" through the Exodus, so Christ conquers rebellious forces in his death. The cross is victory, not defeat.

This cosmic imagery in Colossians 2:14–15 is present within the Christ Hymn. The last line says, "Making peace through his blood, shed on the cross" (Col. 1:20). The song moves from Christ the cosmic Creator to Christ the Redeemer, who puts down cosmic rebellion. Though in conflict with its Creator, Christ reconciles the cosmos with God; the conflict is replaced with *shalom*. The shed blood of the Messiah effected peace.

Jesus holds the "old creation" and the "new creation" together in himself. The second strophe begins with poetic symmetry, as it mirrors the opening line of verse fifteen. Jesus is not only the first-born over creation; he is the firstborn from the dead, the beginning of new creation. Elsewhere Paul says Christ is the "firstborn among many brothers and sisters" (Rom. 8:29) and the "first fruits of those who have fallen asleep" (1 Cor. 15:20). Jesus's resurrection is the harbinger of the forthcoming resurrection harvest: "For in him the fullness of God was pleased to dwell, and through him God was pleased to reconcile to himself all things, whether on earth or in heaven, by making peace through the blood of his cross" (Col. 1:19).

Paul sings how God is pleased to reconcile "all things" in Christ:

Things on earth.
Things in heaven.
All things.

Everything was created through Christ, but rebellious forces enslaved creation. Creation is set free by the one who created it. In order to reconcile it, God overcame the darkness through Christ's blood. If the first half of the song means Christ actually created everything, then the second half means redemption is as cosmic as creation itself. Redemption goes as far as the curse is found.

Inheritance through Christ's Resurrection

The resurrection of the crucified Messiah is a new beginning in the fulfillment of the promises to Abraham. Luke describes the resurrected Jesus so there is no misunderstanding what resurrection means. The skepticism of the disciples provides the opportunity to dismiss any thought of resurrection as the continued life of a disembodied soul. The resurrected Lord commanded the disciples to "*Look* at my hands and my feet; see that it is I myself. *Touch* me and see; for a ghost does not have *flesh and bones* as you see that I have" (Luke 24:39; emphasis ours). Jesus is the model for what resurrection looks like.

The resurrection of the body was a scandal to the Greeks. The philosophers of Athens (Acts 17:32), like the believers in Corinth, were not modern secular humanists. They believed in life after death, but for them it was the soul that was immortal. Paul, however, insisted on bodily resurrection, though philosophers scoffed. Reminding the Corinthians of the gospel (1 Cor. 15:1–4), the apostle insisted the resurrection of the body belongs to the hope of immortality. While the Corinthians did not deny the resurrection of Jesus, even if they misunderstood it, they denied his resurrection had any significance for them. In response, Paul insists the resurrection is a two-stage event. What happened to the Messiah will happen to believers who have died: "But in fact Christ has been raised from the dead, the first fruits of those who have died" (1 Cor. 15:20, 23). Twice Paul identifies Jesus's model resurrection as the "first fruits."

Death is the enemy of God's creation because it is God's enemy (1 Cor. 15:26). The resurrection of Jesus testifies to death's demise, its destruction. Death has been "swallowed up" in the Messiah's bodily resurrection (1 Cor. 15:54–56).

Like Jesus's own resurrection, the resurrection of believers is the redemption of their bodies from death. Some think Paul suddenly "spiritualizes" resurrection because he writes, "Flesh and blood cannot inherit the kingdom of God" (1 Cor. 15:50). Paul, however, has not suddenly embraced the teaching of Plato. In fact, Paul's Jewishness is clear. "Flesh and blood" is a Semitic idiom used two hundred years before Paul in Sirach (Sirach 14:18; 17:31), and it peppers rabbinic literature. The idiom refers to living human beings, not dead ones, in their corrupted Adamic state. These bodies are still subject to sin and death because they are animated by mere "flesh and blood." When the resurrected Messiah appears, God will change the bodies of living disciples into the same kind of victorious body as those who are resurrected (1 Cor. 15:51), just like the body of Jesus, who is the "first fruit."

Consequently, whether we are among the dead raised on that day or among the living that are changed, we all inherit a glorious "spiritual body." This spiritual body is patterned after the resurrection of Jesus. This is not Platonic or Gnostic spiritualism—the body is not a prison for the soul. In fact, the human body is not the problem at all. Sin and death are the problem, and they have corrupted creation and, therefore, our bodies. Through resurrection, our bodies are redeemed from death; our souls are not redeemed from our bodies. Bodies are good. Flesh, as the incarnation declares, is good.

Jesus's resurrection body, with "flesh and bones," is the "spiritual body." The adjective *spiritual* does not refer to the composition of the body but to what makes it "tick." While sin and death are like leaven bringing corruption and decay, the Spirit of God animates resurrected bodies. Just as God's Spirit breathed the breath of life into mud in Genesis 2, so our resurrected body courses with the power of the life-giving Spirit free from corruption, and our bodies thereby share in the honor and dignity of new creation.

Triumph of God's Promise

Paul identifies the goal of the story in Romans, which was written from Cenchreae, a suburb of Corinth. According to Romans 1:2–4, it was

> promised beforehand through his prophets in the holy scriptures,
> the gospel concerning his Son, who was descended from David
> according to the flesh and was declared to be Son of God with
> power according to the spirit of holiness by the resurrection
> from the dead, Jesus Christ our Lord.

For centuries, interpreters have noted chapters five through eight form a tight rhetorical unit in Romans. The magnificent opening in 5:1–11 anticipates the equally majestic conclusion in 8:31–39. The Creator God, who acted in and through the death and resurrection of Jesus on behalf of humanity, even while we were alienated sinners, will certainly act again to deliver the elect. This reconciliation, described in Romans 5:10–11 and Colossians 1, extends to "all things in heaven and on earth." Creation's hope—participating in this reconciling glory—appears climactically in Romans 8.

Drawing on Genesis, Paul believes sin and death vandalized the *shalom* of Eden through the first Adam (Rom. 5:12), and this produced the catastrophic results to which every newspaper testifies. The first Adam brought suffering (Rom. 5:18–21), and creation groans under its effect (Rom. 8:20–23). *Shalom* with God presently exists through faith (Rom. 5:1), yet we live in the hope of the redemption the second Adam extends to the same creation the first Adam ruined.

The resurrection of the dead body of Jesus by the Holy Spirit is good news for God's creation. Death, or the disintegration of Eden, is the work of the first Adam. For Platonists and Gnostics, death is the great liberator because we are freed to return to our pure "spiritual" origin. For Paul, however, death is the enemy. The resurrection of the mortal body of Jesus changed everything: "If the Spirit of him who raised Jesus from the dead is living in you, he who raised Christ from the dead will also give life to your mortal bodies through his Spirit, who lives in you" (Rom. 8:11). The ruin of God's creation, including the human body, is reversed through the work of God, who breathed life into the clay in the beginning. Jesus is the second Adam who accomplishes this reversal through his own death and resurrection (Rom. 5:18–21). Jesus's resurrection is the prototype of our own—the redemption of our bodies (Rom. 8:23)—and this is why Paul calls him the "firstborn from the dead" (Rom. 8:29), the first fruit of the harvest to come.

The "one man, Jesus Christ" reverses what the "one man, Adam" wrought—Jesus is the head of a new humanity, which redeems the old humanity subject to death and corruption (Rom. 5:12–19). For Paul, Jesus is where heaven and earth are reconciled, a salvation-miracle beyond our imagination. The resurrected human, Jesus, is the head of new creation itself.

Those who are baptized into Christ already share in the resurrection as new creatures. Yet we wait. Creation, suffering under human sin since the expulsion from Eden, groans under its burden, sharing in the suffering of humanity. Isaiah bears witness:

> *The earth dries up and withers,*
> *the world languishes and withers;*
> *the heavens languish together with the earth.*
> *The earth lies polluted under its inhabitants;*
> *for they have transgressed the laws,*
> *violated the statutes,*
> *broken the everlasting covenant.*
> *Therefore a curse devours the earth,*
> *and its inhabitants suffer for their guilt;*
> *therefore the inhabitants of the earth swindled,*
> *and few people are left. (Isa. 24:4–6 NRSV)*

Creation is cursed not because it is evil but because the Creator has tied its fate to humanity. Incredibly, binding creation and humanity together was an act of God's hope:

> *For creation was subjected to frustration, not by its own*
> *choice but by the will of the one who subjected it, in hope that*
> *creation itself will be liberated from its bondage to decay and*
> *be brought into the freedom and glory of the children of God.*
> *We know that the whole creation has been groaning, as in the*
> *pains of childbirth right up to the present time. Not only this,*
> *but we ourselves, who have the first fruits of the Spirit, groan*

inwardly as we wait eagerly for our adoption to sonship, the redemption of our bodies. For in this hope we were saved. (Rom. 8:20–24a NIV)

Creation is a significant term in this text. It cannot refer to redeemed believers because "the children of God" is one group distinct from "creation" itself. Creation yearns to experience the "freedom of the glory of the children of God." Neither does it refer to angelic entities because they were never subjected to futility or enslaved to decay. It also does not refer to unbelievers because they are not delivered from the "bondage to decay." Consequently, what Paul means by *creation* is the cosmos, which is Abraham's inheritance (Rom. 4:13). Creation refers to the heavens and the earth, which God subjected to futility in the wake of the original couple's sin. This is the "curse" of Genesis 3. The world God created, though subjected to futility and enslaved to decay, is redeemed—like humanity itself, including "the redemption of our bodies"—from death through the resurrection of Jesus the Messiah.

Creation—the animals, trees, oceans, and skies—is the object of God's redemption through the resurrection of Jesus. Paul knows alternative understandings of salvation (e.g., Plato) but rejects them in light of the death and resurrection of Jesus. At the same time, the redemption of creation is not merely a return to what it once was. Redemption moves creation along to the purposes God had for creation initially. God's creation will be free from sin, free from corruption, and free from death, and thus free to fully become what God intended in the beginning.

Creation cries out—groans—for redemption, to share in the "glory of the children of God" (Rom. 8:21). Believers likewise "wait for adoption, the redemption of our bodies" (Rom. 8:23). Redemption is never *from* the human body. On the contrary, it is the redemption *of* the human body. Creation, human and non-human, is resurrected through the power of God's Holy Spirit to share in the glory of God.

CONCLUSION

The gospel is the story of how God fulfills the promises to Abraham in Jesus the Messiah. The gospel is the hope of Israel, which is resurrection. Resurrection proves God has not given up on creation or its purposes. The gospel is a message of salvation for not only Jews and Gentiles but the whole of creation. It is the message of the resurrected Lord, the resurrection of our mortal human bodies in the power of the Spirit, and the resurrected earth, as the redeemed live in communion with the Triune God. These three wonders are seamlessly sewn together in Paul's biblical narrative.

BULLET POINTS

- The story of redemption narrates God's salvation of both humanity and the world.
- Just as the resurrection of Jesus was material (the "stuff") of creation, so our resurrection will be as well, animated by the Holy Spirit.
- Resurrection is the hope of Israel; it is the gospel given to Abraham and fulfilled in Jesus the Messiah.

QUESTIONS

1. How is the biblical resurrection of the dead different from a Platonic immortality of the soul?

2. Because Paul gives creation a Christological twist, how
   does one's commitment to Christ imply an attitude toward
   creation?

3. How does resurrection tie Jesus, believers, and creation
   together in a seamless thread? Why is this significant?

CHAPTER NINE

Our Inheritance

New Heaven and New Earth

*See, I am making all things new . . . Those who
conquer will inherit these things, and I will be
their God and they will be my children.*

—Revelation 21:5, 7

Inheritance is a dominant theme in God's story. The
words *inherit* or *inheritance* appear almost five hundred times in
the biblical text and most often relate to "land inheritance." Joshua,
for example, uses the language fifty-nine times, primarily in refer-
ence to God's "land grant" to Israel.

The correlation between land and inheritance—between territory and kingdom—runs throughout the plot of the biblical drama.
People cultivate land, kingdoms occupy territory, and the inheritance of the people of God is a new heaven and a new earth.

Abrahamic Promise

When God blessed Abraham, he promised to bless all nations (Gen.
12:2–3). Included in that Abrahamic blessing is the land promise:
"I will give this land to your offspring" (Gen. 12:7).

This promise is both *overplayed*, as some identify the contemporary state of Israel with this land, and *undervalued*, as others see no fulfillment in Israel's Messiah. The former think the state of Israel is its fulfillment (or at least its beginning), while the latter believe the land promise no longer applies. There is a third way.

The land is Israel's inheritance as the firstborn child of God among the nations (Ex. 32:13; Lev. 20:24; Num. 4:20). God gave the "land for an inheritance to Israel" (Josh. 11:23). One need only skim the Torah, especially Deuteronomy, to recognize the central role land plays as the inheritance Israel receives from Yahweh as God's child (e.g., Deut. 4:21; cf. Ps. 136:21–22).

As part of the Abrahamic promise, the land is not conditioned by the Mosaic covenant because the promise came before the law (Gal. 3:6–9). The "inheritance" is received by faith rather than by the works of the Torah (Gal. 3:17–18). God intends to fulfill the promise to Abraham whether Israel ever keeps the covenant or not. Israel's possession of the land at any particular time in history is conditioned by their obedience to the Mosaic covenant, but the ultimate fulfillment of the Abrahamic promise is unqualified. It is as unconditional as the promise of the Messiah. While Israel may or may not occupy the land throughout its history due to their obedience or sin, ultimately and finally, "the meek will inherit the earth" (Matt. 5:5 KJV).

God gives land and God gives rest (Josh. 11:23). "Rest" is what God gives to Israel when they seek Yahweh (2 Chron. 14:1, 5–6; 20:30; 23:21), and rest means "no war" (2 Chron. 14:5). "Rest" reappears in the prophets as Israel's hope. The righteous will rest, but the wicked will not (Isa. 14:7; 30:15; 32:17; 57:20). Ultimately, God's people will rest in the land without fear (Jer. 30:10; 46:27). Both Isaiah and Micah see a time when the nations will no longer train for war, the earth will be at peace, and no one will be afraid (Isa. 2:1–4; Mic. 4:1–5). The earth has not yet experienced this. We are still waiting for that day.

This language echoes God's purpose in creation. God's land grant to Israel is analogous to God's gift of the earth to humanity when God "rested" humanity (Gen. 2:15) in the Garden to serve and protect it. Adam and Eve were priests in God's temple, God's home. This is God's inheritance for humanity.

The land grant to Israel is ultimately eschatological. God creates the new heaven and new earth as an inheritance for redeemed humanity. What Israel inherited in the book of Joshua typifies the inheritance God will give to humanity. A day is coming when Israel is not the only "heritage" of God, but Egypt and Assyria are God's people and heirs as well (Isa. 19:25). A day is coming when the meek will inherit the earth (Matt. 5:5).

Prophetic Expectations

Psalm 37 illustrates how the hope of inheriting the land, living in the land, and experiencing God's goodness in the land is integral to Israel's joy in the Lord. Disturbed by the prosperity of the wicked, the psalmist assures Israel that those who hope in the Lord will inherit the land. Six times the psalmist promises—and liturgically rehearses—that Israel will ultimately receive its promised inheritance. They will "inherit the land" (Ps. 37:22, 29). Jesus quotes Psalm 37:11 when he announces: "Blessed are the meek for they shall inherit the earth" (Matt. 5:5 KJV).

This enduring hope of "inheriting the earth," a renewal of creation, is pervasive in the prophetic literature. The prophetic message of hope envisioned a "new heaven and a new earth" (Isa. 65:17). God's commitment to the land pervades Israel's hope.

That same message resonates with disciples of Jesus. While the present is filled with "times of refreshing" from the presence of the Holy Spirit, the future brings a "the time for restoring all things about which God spoke by the mouth of his holy prophets long ago" (Acts 3:20–21). Here are a few representative prophets where land renewal is prominent:

> "I will plant Israel in their land,
>   never again to be uprooted
>   from the land that I have given them," says the LORD your God.
>   (Amos 9:15 NIV)

> Instead of the thornbush will grow the juniper,
>   and instead of briers the myrtle will grow.
>   This will be for the Lord's renown, for an everlasting sign, that
>   will endure forever. (Isa. 55:13 NIV)

> The Lord will be king over all the earth;
>   and his name the only name . . .

> It will be inhabited; never again will it be destroyed.
>   Jerusalem will be secure. (Zech. 14:9, 11 NIV)

The most stirring text, which New Testament writers echo, is Isaiah 65:17–25:

> "See, I will create
>   new heavens and a new earth.
>   The former things will not be remembered,
>   nor will they come to mind. But be glad and rejoice forever
>   in what I will create,
>   for I will create Jerusalem to be a delight
>   and its people a joy. I will rejoice over Jerusalem

and take delight in my people;
the sound of weeping and of crying
will be heard in it no more.

"Never again will there be in it an infant who lives but a few days,
or an old man who does not live out his years;
the one who dies at a hundred
will be thought a mere child;
the one who fails to reach a hundred
will be considered accursed.
They will build houses and dwell in them;
they will plant vineyards and eat their fruit.
No longer will they build houses and others live in them,
or plant and others eat.
For as the days of a tree,
so will be the days of my people;
my chosen ones will long enjoy
the work of their hands.
They will not labor in vain,
nor will they bear children doomed to misfortune;
for they will be a people blessed by the Lord,
they and their descendants with them.
Before they call I will answer;
while they are still speaking I will hear.
The wolf and the lamb will feed together,
and the lion will eat straw like the ox,
and dust will be the serpent's food.
They will neither harm nor destroy
on all my holy mountain," says the Lord. (NIV)

The elderly and children are supported rather than abandoned, everyone has appropriate shelter and housing, everyone is employed with meaningful work, everyone has adequate food and drink, children are blessed, creation will live in *shalom* with itself, and chaos—the serpent—will disappear in the dust. This is accomplished by the work of the Messiah (Isa. 11:1–9).

Heirs of the Promise

Galatians 3 argues the promise was made before the Torah existed and is, therefore, not conditioned by Torah obedience. Israel will inherit the land as God promised Abraham, and God is faithful. Paul explicitly states, "It was not through the law that Abraham and his offspring received the promise" (Rom. 4:13).

This is a significant point. The Abrahamic promise belongs to the children of Israel. The land is part of the Abrahamic promise. The children of Israel will possess the land; it is their inheritance. It is an unconditional promise.

But who is Israel? Who are the children of Abraham? Because the "promise comes by faith," it is "guaranteed to all Abraham's offspring—not only to those who are of the law" (e.g., Torah-obeying ethnic Israel) "but also to those who have the faith of Abraham" (e.g., including the nations). In this sense, Abraham is the "father of many nations"—he is the "father of us all" (Rom. 4:16–17). The Gentiles (nations) have been grafted into Israel through faith (Rom. 11:17). Those who belong to the Messiah are the children of Abraham and thus "heirs" of the promise (Gal. 3:29). Renewed Israel includes Jews and Gentiles, and together they constitute the "Israel of God" as part of God's "new creation" (Gal. 6:15–16).

But does this include the land? Yes, it does. Abraham was the "heir of the world" (cosmos), not just the land of Palestine (Rom. 4:13). The inheritance of the children of Abraham is heaven and earth.

We do not obtain this land by violence or purchase. We receive it by faith in the Messiah and on the ground of the Messiah's faithfulness. The "faith[fulness] of Jesus" secures the inheritance for Israel, and we participate in it through faith (Gal. 3:22). The Messiah is the heir of the all things, and we are coheirs with the Messiah through faith (Rom. 8:17).

Creation is our inheritance. We wait, according to Romans 8:18–25, for the full adoption into the family of God when our bodies are redeemed (resurrection) and creation is liberated (new heaven and new earth). That is our inheritance. John echoes the whole Abrahamic trajectory (Gen. 17:7–8) in Revelation: "*Those who are victorious will inherit all this*, and I will be their God and they will be my children" (21:7; emphasis ours).

The Abrahamic promise was first given to ethnic Israel but, by faith and because of the Messiah, it includes the nations as well. Perhaps on the new heaven and new earth, the redeemed of ethnic Israel will dwell in Palestine—in the land between the rivers of Egypt and Babylon—but the whole earth will belong to the people of God as they again reign on the earth with God. The kingdom of God will fill the earth!

This accounts for Paul's pervasive "inheritance" language. He writes about inheriting "the kingdom of God" (1 Cor. 6:9–10; Gal. 5:21; Eph. 5:5). He praises God for gifting us with the Spirit as a down payment of our inheritance, which will arrive when God has fully redeemed God's treasured possession (Eph. 1:14). Through faith, Paul writes, we are "qualified to share in the inheritance of the saints in the kingdom of light" (Col. 1:12).

The fullness of the kingdom of God, which is yet to come, is our inheritance. It is the final fulfillment of the Abrahamic promise through which God will make Israel a great nation, a great name, and bless all the nations. That promise, including the whole cosmos, belongs to all those who place their hope in God's Messiah.

Consequently, the new heaven and new earth (creation renewed) is integral to the plot line of the story of God from creation through Abraham to new creation. The earth is the inheritance of God's people, and one day the reign of God will fill it from the east to the west, from the north to the south. The whole earth, unlike its present condition, will become "Holy to the Lord" (Zech. 14:20).

Inheriting the (New) Earth

At a climactic moment in the drama of Revelation, "loud voices in heaven" announce,

> *The kingdom of this world has become*
> *the kingdom of our Lord and of his Messiah,*
> *and he will reign forever and ever. (Rev. 11:15)*

This evokes gratitude and worship from those who surround the throne of God. They "give thanks" because the Lord God Almighty has "begun to reign." This reign involves the judging of the dead, the rewarding of the saints, and—significantly for our purposes— "*destroying those who destroy the earth*" (Rev. 11:16–18; emphasis ours).

Here *earth* does not refer to people because the Apocalypse habitually refers to the "inhabitants of the earth" as such. This refers to creation. The Creator of "heaven and earth, the sea and the springs of water" (Rev. 14:7) judges those who destroy the earth God created. This is one reason creation itself worships God, as "every creature in heaven and on earth and under the earth and in the sea, and all that is in them" give "blessing and honor and glory and might forever and ever" to the Lamb and the one who sits on the throne (Rev. 5:13).

When the "destroyers of earth" are judged, the saints are redeemed. When the earth is avenged, creation rejoices. When the kingdom of God fills the earth, the redeemed "from every tribe and language and people and nation" will become ministering priests and "reign on the earth" (Rev. 5:10).

God's dramatic story reaches its goal in Revelation 21–22. The climatic picture is wondrous:

> *Then I saw a new heaven and a new earth, for the first heaven*
> *and the first earth had passed away, and the sea was no more.*
> *And I saw the holy city, the new Jerusalem, coming down out of*
> *heaven from God, prepared as a bride adorned for her husband.*
> *And I heard a loud voice from the throne saying,*
>
> > *"Behold, the home of God is among mortals.*
> > *He will dwell with them as their God;*
> > *they will be his peoples,*
> > *and God himself will be with them;*
> > *he will wipe every tear from their eyes.*
> > *Death will be no more;*
> > *mourning and crying and pain will be no more,*
> > *for the first things have passed away."*
>
> *And the one who was seated on the throne said, "See, I am making all*
> *things new." (Rev. 21:1–5a)*

"New heaven and new earth" echoes the story of creation in Genesis 1–3. The echo, however, is no mere restoration of creation. Rather, it is a transformation, or transfiguration, of the present, old creation into something new.

Though chaos remains in the old creation, chaos will disappear in the new. Darkness—part of the original chaos in Genesis 1:2—will no longer exist in the new creation, since "the glory of God is its light" (Rev. 21:23; cf. 22:5). The waters of the deep, representing chaos, were part of the old creation, but in the new there will be no more sea (Rev. 21:1). "The sea is no more" assures chaos no longer exists.[1] The consequences of tragic human choices, described in Genesis 3, no longer exist in the new creation—death, mourning, and pain disappear (Rev. 21:4). Indeed, the curse of Genesis 3 is removed (Rev. 22:3). Chaos no longer poses any threat to creation. The earth will never again suffer from human choices or chaotic forces.

Everything chaos and sin produce in the present, old world—death, mourning, pain—will disappear in the new one. The old world will pass away, everything will be made new, and the new world will emerge as a place where God dwells with humanity. What God has prepared for us in heaven (God's dwelling place) will descend to the new earth under the new heavens in the new creation. God will again dwell with humanity, just as God did in Eden.

But Eden is no longer one place on the earth. Rather, Eden fills the earth. The whole creation, unlike in Eden, is God's sanctuary—the Holy of Holies. The new city is a perfect cube, just like the Holy of Holies in Israel's temple. There is no temple on the new earth because the cosmos itself is the temple of God.

The city in Revelation 21–22 stands in contrast to the great city of Babylon in Revelation 17–18. While the latter is filled with greed and immorality, the former excludes all sinfulness. While the latter has dominated and ruled the earth as "the kingdom of this world" since humanity's expulsion from Eden, the new Jerusalem will fulfill all the hopes of the prophets and the Abrahamic promise. In the new Jerusalem, the nations are healed and blessed, provisions are abundant, and the tree and water of life are in the midst of the new earth forever.

Does God create ex nihilo, out of nothing, like in the original creation? Is the old creation annihilated and then a totally different world created? We don't think so.

God's promise is "See, I am making all things new" (Rev. 21:5). The text does not say God will make new things. Rather, God will make all things new. This is restoration, healing, and renewal.

CONCLUSION

This is a new beginning. It is renewal. It is new creation. It is analogous to new life after the flood, or a new Exodus when Israel entered the Promised Land. The new earth is our inheritance, and God invites the redeemed "to inherit these things," where God will be our God and we will be God's children (Rev. 21:7). This is our inheritance.

BULLET POINTS

- God unconditionally promised Abraham's descendants they would inherit the whole cosmos.
- Christians are Abraham's descendants and therefore heirs of that promise.
- The meek will inherit the earth when everything is made new in the new heaven and new earth.

QUESTIONS

1. Does the Abraham promise include the land such that Abraham is the "heir of the cosmos?" What does it mean for Christians to recognize they are "heirs" of the Abrahamic promise?

2. Are the prophetic hopes of Israel all fulfilled in the present age, or is there a fuller experience of this hope in the age to come?

3. What is new about the "new heaven" and "new earth," and what does it mean for the "old" to "pass away"?

Part II

Living the Narrative

CHAPTER TEN

Practicing Resurrection

Living God's New Creation

*The practice of resurrection is an intentional, deliberate
decision to believe and participate in resurrection
life, life out of death, life that trumps death.*
—Eugene Peterson[1]

In a series of parables about sowing seeds, wheat
among weeds, mustard seeds, and finding things, Jesus stressed
spiritual discernment: "Let anyone with ears listen!" (Matt. 13:9).
Jesus concludes, "Have you understood all this?" Everyone who
does "is like the master of a household who brings out of his treasure what is old and new," trained for the kingdom of God (Matt.
13:51–52).

More than knowing the "facts" of the word, Jesus wants people
to understand what God is doing in the Messiah. He questions
whether we understand the story well enough to live in the present
as scribes trained in the kingdom. Similarly, in light of a coming
new world, Peter asks, "What kind [of] people ought [we] to be?"
He answers we ought to "strive to be found by him at peace, without
spot or blemish" (2 Peter 3:11, 14).

We pray this book contributes to that goal. We believe its thrust, if faithful to Scripture, encourages an obedient life. We are called to live in the present as new creatures, a part of God's new creation. In other words, we *practice* resurrection now because we already share in the resurrection of Jesus, participate in the resurrected new humanity, and breathe the air of the resurrected world.

Practice Resurrection by Remembering Our Story

Interpreters disagree about the most frequent command. Is it some form of "do not be afraid" or "remember"? Whatever the case, remembering frequently counters fear. Deuteronomy repeatedly calls Israel to faithful memory:

> "Remember the day you stood before the LORD." (Deut. 4:10)
> "Remember that you were slaves in Egypt." (Deut. 5:15)
> "Do not be afraid . . . remember what the LORD your God did." (Deut. 7:18)
> "Remember how the LORD your God led you." (Deut. 8:2)
> "Remember what the LORD your God did." (Deut. 24:9)

Faithfulness to the greatest commandment, which is to love the Lord with our whole being (Deut. 6:4), is connected to memory and forgetfulness. Israel recites it and puts it on doorposts—even on their foreheads—so they will not forget the Lord redeemed them from slavery (Deut. 6:12). "When your children ask you in time to come, 'What is the meaning of the decrees?'" (Deut. 6:20), the parent tells the story of God's gracious salvation of Abraham's descendants (Deut. 6:21–25). That story has one star—the Creator God, who called Israel to fulfill creation's purposes. Grace is center stage in the story, as God chose the smallest, most stubborn, and most marginalized people to bless the nations and the world (Deut. 7:7–9; 9:4–6).

The story fosters obedience. When we remember the story, we love God and remain true to God's purposes. When we forget the story, we forget God's purposes and who we are. The story defines identity.

God's people learned the story primarily through corporate worship. Each Sabbath, Jewish families gathered in joyous celebration of the gifts of creation and redemption. On that day, they were set free from bondage to enjoy the freedom God bestowed upon the world in the beginning. The cadence of life conformed to the rhythm of God's story.

In the festivals, Israel marked time with the story of grace. The Passover with its special aromas, entrées, and questions reminded Israel that God had liberated them from bondage and situated them *in* the story of God's salvation. Each one of Israel's festivals tells the story of God and their place within it. The festivals reminded Israel of what God had done in the past and what God is doing in the present. Israel practiced faithfulness by knowing the story. As the festivals rehearsed the story, they shared its meaning.

We also belong to that narrative. Disciples of Jesus are neither disconnected nor separated from the story remembered in the *Shema*, the Sabbath, and the festivals. It is our story, too!

We participate in the same narrative through baptism, which embodies the story of God healing a fractured world. Baptism tells the story of a people where race, language, and gender do not define community. Baptism announces God's new creation has arrived, fulfilling the promises to Abraham. Gentiles, by virtue of belonging to the Messiah, have been baptized into Israel's narrative (Gal. 3:27–29). God's faithfulness to Israel gives the Galatians an identity in Christ. Paul writes, "*If* you belong to Christ, *then* you are Abraham's offspring, heirs according to the promise" (Gal. 3:29; emphasis ours). Baptism binds Jews and Gentiles to the same covenant—God's covenant with Abraham.

Christians continue the weekly proclamation of the story through a meal. The Lord's Supper flows out of the Passover, and the table embodies its meaning. We not only celebrate our liberation from Egypt but we, climatically, celebrate the culmination of redemption's story. Jesus, like Moses, insisted we "do" this in his memory (Luke 22:19).

What is the story? What is the hinge on which everything else swings? What must we have eyes to see and ears to hear?

- God lovingly created the world as a home in which to dwell.
- God commissioned humanity as royal priests to protect and serve Eden, but humanity rebelled against the Creator.
- God graciously chose Abraham and his descendants, representative of all nations, as the vehicle for the redemption of all creation.
- God initiated the reclamation of creation in the incarnation, ministry, death, resurrection, and enthronement of the Messiah.
- God renews humanity in the restoration of Israel, honoring his covenants to Abraham and David.
- God fulfills creation's purposes through the great victory of Jesus's ministry and resurrection by judging sin and death, purifying creation, and dwelling with the resurrected Jesus and saints in the renewed creation.

This is the story. It is told over and over in Scripture, on the Sabbath, at the festivals, in our baptism, and in the Lord's Supper. It is the narrative in which we find ourselves. We remember and live that story.

Remembering the story gives us identity. We are the focus of infinite love. We are creatures like every living thing. We are royal priests who serve and protect God's treasure, creation (it's like we were given the keys to a '57 Chevy for safekeeping!). We are redeemed, adopted, and formed as temples of God's glory. We are reconciled to God, to creation, and to each other. We live faithfully as God's holy people when we remember this story.

We practice resurrection by remembering and embodying God's narrative—the resurrection of the Messiah, the resurrection of God's people, and the resurrection of God's world.

Becoming Fully Human in Caring for Creation

God, through Christ, created the world. Creation is intrinsically good, and this goodness is not based on its utility for humans. The Creator declares creation "good" six times before humanity exists. Humanity shares in the goodness of creation and is placed within creation as royal priests to care for God's garden.

Humanity and the world are bound together by God. Everything exists for the praise of God's glory. The goal of a Christ-centered life does not happen apart from the rest of God's creation. Glorifying God is a vocation we share with all creation. We praise God with our hearts, hands, and voices; with our minds as well as our emotions; with art and music. In other words, we glorify God by becoming what we were created to be. We fulfill our role as God's priests by enabling creation to become what God created it to be.

On one level, it does not matter if "global warming" is real or imagined, caused by nature or humans. Caring for God's good world is a matter of obedience and discipleship. We are responsible to Christ, the redeemer and heir of all creation, for the following:

- The pollution of the earth's water, skies, and land
- The greed-fueled destruction of rainforest and coastal wetlands complexes
- The trophy hunting or poaching of rare animals approaching extinction

If the Father is mindful of the death of even a single sparrow (Matt. 10:29), then we, who reflect the divine image, will care as well.

When we care for creation, we exercise the royal priestly function for which we were created. Becoming a Christian does not free us from the mandate given to original humanity. Quite the contrary—Christ restores our true identity as humans invested with responsibility for creation.

The modern world is dominated by the supreme cultural value of making money. In response, we practice resurrection by condemning the rape of creation because of human greed and injustice. Caring for creation is a prophetic vocation for God's people, who live as aliens and exiles in the present age. As people of reconciliation, we live together in God's world for the good of humans and nonhumans.

Consequently, in caring for God's creation, we exercise the divine traits of compassion and justice. We practice Godlike selfless love when we care for one of God's creatures, which can never return the favor. God's unrequited love for birds, grass, and flowers assures us of the Father's unending love for us. Psalm 145 links God's compassion, dominion, and justice together. The Lord has "compassion on all that he has made . . . your dominion endures forever . . . The LORD is just in all his ways" (Ps. 145:9, 13, 17). Correspondingly, how we respect God's animals is a sign of righteousness: "The righteous man cares for the needs of his animals" (Prov. 12:10 NIV).

When we care for God's creation, we practice resurrection by testifying to God's redemptive healing of creation through the Messiah's victory.

Practicing *Shalom* and Hospitality

God's kingdom is about peace and hospitality (Rom. 15:17). In the act of creation, God welcomed the world into God's own life and blessed it with *shalom*. But human rebellion ravaged the reign of peace with wars between races, sexes, and ranks.

The history of redemption is the history of extending and restoring *shalom* and hospitality within creation. The most astonishing miracle in the Exodus is not the parting of the Red Sea but how God welcomed the Israelite delegation with a banquet on the mountain where they "saw the God of Israel" and "ate and drank" (Ex. 24:9–11). Isaiah envisions that banquet in God's coming kingdom. It is a feast "for all peoples" full of "rich food" and "well-aged wine." The table celebrates the destruction of death (Isa. 25:6–10a).

Jesus restores *shalom* and hospitality through his Jubilee ministry. Welcoming strangers at the table, he concretely proclaimed a reality inaugurated through his death and resurrection. *Shalom*-making is the essential message of the cross, and it ends the ethnic divisions between Jew and Gentile:

> For he is our peace; in his flesh he has made both groups into
> one and has broken down the dividing wall, that is, the hostility
> between us . . . that he might create one new humanity in place

> *of the two, thus making peace, and might reconcile both groups*
> *to God in one body through the cross, thus putting to death that*
> *hostility through it. So he came and proclaimed peace to you*
> *who were far off and peace to those who were near; for through*
> *him both of us have access in one Spirit to the Father.*
> *(Eph. 2:14–18)*

Peace is not a "byproduct" of the gospel. *Shalom* is the heart of the mission of God in Christ. The Messiah reconciles the world to God (Eph. 1:10). Jesus preached peace. Jesus made peace.

This is not an abstract idea. *Shalom*, a dynamic movement of God, dictates behavior in the kingdom. When Peter, led by the Spirit, went to Cornelius's house, he preached "peace by Jesus Christ—Lord of all" (Acts 10:36). *Shalom* erased the gulf between Jew and Gentile. Peace was concretely realized as Jews and Gentiles ate at the same table (Acts 11:1–18), a table of *shalom* and welcome.

Practicing *shalom* welcomes strangers. As in creation, the table values diversity. We practice hospitality to welcome God's diverse creation ("every nation, tribes and peoples and languages" [Rev. 7:9]) and to embody the ministry of Jesus. The practice of *shalom* does not arise out of a spirit of condescension or pity. Rather, it recognizes the dignity and equal worth of every person, which is rooted in both creation and redemption.

We recognize a person's value through the lens of creation and redemption. Both God and Christ are mediated to us in every person, including those some regard as second or third class. We do not look at any person as flawed cultures do. Rather, through baptized eyes, we see the reality of new creation (Matt. 25:31–46). Recognizing Jesus in the poor, the outsider, and the sinner radically alters Christian vision. We welcome each of these precisely because each is Christ, and God values each one as a divine image.

Whatever else people do, if they do not practice *shalom* and hospitality, they cannot be the people of God. The stunning reality of former Ku Klux Klansmen and Black Panthers sharing a meal together because of Jesus embodies and exemplifies new creation. The early followers of the way understood the radical nature of hospitality. *Shalom* flows from the table of plenty and into the community around us. Eating at God's table is not limited to Sunday morning. Hospitality was among the most effective "mission" agendas in the first centuries of God's restored Israel.

Through their practice of *shalom* and hospitality, early believers recognized Jesus in each of society's down-and-outs. They heralded a new creation where there is neither Jew nor Greek, male nor female, rich nor poor. They practiced resurrection by being people of *shalom*.

CONCLUSION

Practicing resurrection comes naturally to people whose identity is shaped by God's restoration narrative. When we know God's story, we are able to discern our place in it. The narrative reveals our responsibility to take care of the world Christ created and redeems. Those who believe the gospel embrace a deliberate decision to act as if God's new creation in Jesus has already arrived.

BULLET POINTS

- God's people practice resurrection because they believe a specific story about the world.
- Practicing resurrection involves adopting a specific posture toward God, creation, and humanity.

- Practicing resurrection permeates God's people as the aroma of the new creation breaks into this world through us.

QUESTIONS

1. What is the correlation between living by faith and remembering God's story? In what ways do we remember God's story?

2. What are some concrete ways in which Christians might protect God's creation as an act of devotion and faith in its resurrection?

3. How might your congregation practice *shalom* and welcoming?

CHAPTER ELEVEN

Creation, New Creation, and the Sacraments

Baptism, Lord's Supper, and Assembly

In the history of Christianity there exist two primary patterns of conceiving of God's relationship to the world and of ordering Christian faith and practice in light of this conception: sacramental Christianity and Christian Gnosticism. There are of course various places on a continuum between these two primary patterns. But the extent to which a particular Christian tradition is non-sacramental is the extent to which that tradition is ultimately Gnostic in the way it conceives of God's relationship to the world and orders its faith and practice accordingly.

—Steven R. Harmon and Paul Avis[1]

We recognize that "sacramental theology" carries negative baggage for many. We could avoid this language, but there are reasons to emphasize the *sacramental* character of Baptism, the Lord's Supper, and Assembly.[2]

If "sacrament" means some kind of ritualistic power rooted in institutionalism or clerical authority, then we are not interested. If "sacrament" has overtones of "magical powers" or "superstition," we are not interested in that, either. If "sacrament" entails faith is unnecessary or the ritualistic act itself (in terms of its own power) imparts grace, then we are certainly not interested. However, "sacrament" does not necessarily mean any of those things. Wherever those ideas are present, they are layers placed on top of the central idea of sacramental theology.

That central idea is that God acts through appointed, material means to impart grace, assurance, and hope. We prefer "sacrament" to "ordinance" precisely because we want to emphasize that God works through these means.

Popular Christianity is often human-centered in its approach to Baptism, the Lord's Supper, and Assembly. The "ordinances" are often regarded as mere acts of human obedience. They are primarily, if not exclusively, something *we do*. Stressing sacramentality, however, need not undermine the "ordinance" function—that is, obedience. Rather, stressing sacramentality moves toward a more God-centered understanding, recognizing them as divine acts of grace.

How might we think about Christian "ordinances" as "sacraments"? Instead of polarizing the two designations, perhaps *together* they embrace the fullness of what God has invested in Baptism, the Lord's Supper, and Assembly.

Definition of a Sacrament

The Latin word *sacramentum* is sometimes translated as "pledge" or "mystery." Both meanings have advocates, and both are appropriate. However, the mystery of the sacrament is more fundamental than its pledging function. The sacraments are more than simple "church ordinances." Their pledging function is significant *because* they are divine mysteries. The power of the sacrament is God's work, which we embrace through faith.

When viewed primarily or solely as human pledge, "sacramental" theology is anthropocentric because it prioritizes what *we do*—we pledge allegiance, we testify to God's grace, we obey, we remember, we gather. But sacrament as mystery is theocentric because it emphasizes what *God does*—God acts through the sacraments by the Spirit through faith. Both perspectives are important, but divine action grounds and gives meaning to our obedience. They not only signify and bear witness to the gospel; they are also concrete, material *means* within time and space through which God communicates grace to believers.

Sacraments are material (creational) realities, and they represent the reality of the gospel—that is, they are concrete signs pointing beyond themselves to the work of God in Christ. But they do more than point; they are means of grace that participate in the reality to which they point and are joined to that reality by the promise of God's word. This experience is eschatological, as we participate in the present-yet-future reality of the kingdom of God. We are raised with Christ through Baptism, eat with Jesus at the Messianic banquet, and assemble around the throne of God. The power of this sacramental moment, however, is not contained in the sign itself but is effected by the Spirit, who mediates the presence of God through the sacrament as we receive what God gives through faith. The ground of God's gracious acts in the sacraments is the reconciling work of Christ through his incarnation, ministry, death, resurrection, and enthronement. The sacraments, then, are triune in faith and practice.

The sacraments are a human witness to the grace of God as well as a human pledge of allegiance to the story of God in Jesus. They are also divine pledges of assurance and means by which God encounters, communes with, and transforms believers into the image of Christ.

Sacramental Foundations in the Story of God

The sacraments are present throughout redemptive history. God's story is a sacramental journey, analogous to a five-act drama—a *theodrama*.

Act One: Creation

Some reject sacramental mystery because it involves material objects. Nothing external or physical, it is said, can mediate the spiritual. Ultimately, this denies the goodness of creation. Creation is God's temple. God rested in creation and was present through the tree of life, through walking in the Garden, and sharing life with humanity. Materiality does not hinder communion with God but mediates it. We experience something of this through nature walks, watching falling snow, siting on cliffs overlooking the ocean, or watching a beautiful sunset. We feel God's presence in such moments.

Act Two: Israel

While some dismiss the "externals" and "ceremonies" of Israel, these were sacramental occasions of God's presence within Israel. The temple, for example, was no mere symbol of divine presence; it was truly God's communing presence, though it could not contain God's fullness. Circumcision sealed the promise of God, Israel's sacrifices mediated forgiveness, the meals at which they ate the sacrifices were occasions for rejoicing before the Lord, and their assemblies "saw" God. Though fulfilled in Christ, they were nevertheless authentic experiences of divine presence.

Act Three: Christ

The theological root of sacramental theology is Christ, the sacrament of God. The incarnation sanctified creation—God became flesh, and flesh mediated God's presence to the world. God in the flesh affirms materiality. The fullness of God dwelt in the physical body of Jesus. To polarize materiality and spirituality is to undermine the incarnation, where the material and spiritual are united in the person of Jesus. The sacraments draw their meaning, power, and efficacy from the union of God and creation in the incarnation. They are fundamentally Christological rather than ecclesiological, since Jesus himself is sacrament. If flesh and deity are united in Jesus, God can unite materiality and grace in Baptism, the Lord's Supper, and Assembly. Indeed, the latter is grounded in the former.

Moreover, Jesus himself, as the Incarnate God, participated in Israel's sacramental journey. He was baptized with Israel, assembled with Israel in its festive celebrations (Sabbaths, Passovers, Feasts of Tabernacles), and ate at those tables. Jesus practiced Israel's sacraments. More than that, he gave them new meaning, depth, and significance. Jesus did not discontinue the sacramental journey. On the contrary, he kicked it up a notch.

Act Four: Church

As the "second incarnation" of Jesus in the world, the church is itself a sacramental reality as the body of Christ. Baptized in the Spirit, God dwells in its members. We—finite, embodied people—are the habitation of God. This is no figure of speech. We are sacramental beings; we live each moment as divine dwelling places.

Act Five: Eschaton

Though the church is flawed by its own sin, she is the body of Christ and remains an authentic sacrament of God's presence. This eschatological community of God will enjoy entire sanctification in both spirit and body in the new heaven and new earth. The Spirit of God will transform our bodies from mortality into immortality. We will live on the new earth in spiritual bodies—that is, material bodies animated by the Spirit of God. Our resurrected, immortal bodies will be sacramental dwelling places of God's Spirit, and God will fully rest in the new creation.

This is God's overarching, sacramental story—the sacraments exist as God's gifts to the church. Through them, we savor the future, which assures and confirms our present faith. In the sacraments, the future becomes present. That future is new creation, begun in the resurrection of Jesus and shared with us in the sacraments. The sacraments mark our journey of faith from creation to new creation.

High Drama in Community: Baptism, the Lord's Supper, and Assembly

Baptism, the Lord's Supper, and Assembly are dramatic rehearsals of the story through which God renews communion, empowers transformation, and realizes the future. By faith, the community participates in this story through water, food and drink, and gatherings in the power of the Spirit.

These gospel sacraments/ordinances have ordinarily (though with some variation) been construed in this way: (1) Baptism as the means of grace for justification through participation in the death and resurrection of Jesus, (2) the Lord's Supper as a means of grace for sanctification through remembrance and communion with the death of Christ, and (3) the Lord's day (Assembly) as a means of grace for communal worship through celebration of the resurrection (new creation). In this sense, they are testimonies to the gospel as "ordinances," and they are also sacramental means through which believers experience the grace of the gospel in the Spirit. In other words, these gospel symbols mediate the presence of Christ to his community. They are both ordinances and sacraments!

They are not substitutes for discipleship or transformation. Rather, they are moments of divine-human encounters through the creative work of God's sanctifying Spirit. This kind of sacramentalism is not popular. Many empty all sacramental imagination from these ordinances. Baptism becomes either a mere symbol or a test of loyalty. The Lord's Supper becomes an anthropocentric form of individualistic piety. Assembly becomes either a legal test of faithfulness or a mere occasion for mutual encouragement, susceptible to pragmatic consumerism.

In *Enter the Water, Come to the Table: Baptism and the Lord's Supper in God's Story of New Creation*, John Mark Hicks suggested the Lord's Supper is an authentic communion with God through Christ in the power of the Spirit, and Baptism is a means of grace through which we encounter the saving act of God in Christ through his death and resurrection. Further, in *A Gathered People*, Hicks and Bobby Valentine with Johnny Melton suggested Assembly, wherever and whenever a community of Christ-followers gathers to seek God's face, participates in the eschatological Assembly because the Spirit ushers us into the heavenly Jerusalem where we share the future with all the saints gathered around the world and throughout time. Baptism, the Lord's Supper, and Assembly are moments of communion, participation, and encounter.

Baptism, Lord's Supper, and Assembly: Old and New Creation

Created materiality is good; indeed, it is "very good." It is delightful and wondrous. God created the world as a temple in which to dwell, a place where God and humanity would enjoy each other, delight in the wonder of the cosmos, care for it, and rest within it. We participate in the communion of God's life through materiality. Creation is not an addendum or a secondary reality but a means by which humanity experiences God's Spirit and feeds our own spirituality.

But alas, creation is now broken. It is still good, but broken. It is enslaved, infected with unruly chaos and pervasive sin, and groans along with humanity for liberation from its bondage. Nevertheless, creation still serves its function. We still experience God through creation when, for example, we enjoy the beauty of a sunset. We experience God in its little things as well as in its majestic views. Yet creation is frustrated. It is filled with pain, tragedy, and death. Like the cosmos itself, we are frustrated and yearn for redemption.

Despite its brokenness, God affirmed the goodness of creation through the Christ Event, which inaugurated new humanity. The Son is new creation, the second Adam, the new human. Because of the Messiah's work, the sacraments are places where the new creation breaks into the old one. They are moments where God provides a taste of new creation.

Baptism is more than just a regular dip in water. We may experience God in the shower, through a long hot bath, or by a swim in the ocean. Old creation is still good and still mediates God's presence. But Baptism is more.

Baptism is the watershed of new creation in a believer's life. The water of the old creation becomes a means by which we experience the new. It is still water—created materiality is not annihilated—but it also participates in the reality of the new creation through our union with Christ. Through Baptism we participate in the death and resurrection of Jesus. We rise from the watery grave to live as signposts of the new creation. Baptism is a new creation bath with old creation water. It ushers us, by the Spirit, into the heavenly throne room where we are seated with Christ at the right hand of God (Eph. 2:6). In Baptism, we experience our future resurrection as if it has already happened. Death has no claim upon us because we have been baptized. We are new creatures in Christ.

Assembly is more than a mere gathering of people—it is not simply a group of people "hanging out." We may experience God through table talk at Starbucks, going to ballgames, and playing together in God's good creation. Old creation is good and still mediates God's presence in the world. But Assembly is more.

Assembly is the experience of new creation. The gathering of God's people within the old creation becomes a means by which we experience the reality of new creation. Though still living in this broken, old creation, this gathering of embodied creatures participates in the reality of the new creation through union with the eschatological Assembly around the throne of God, pictured in Revelation 7:9–17. Through Assembly we enter the Holy of Holies as a community drawn from every nation, language, and tribe, and we join the community already gathered there—the saints who have gone before us. We join the angelic chorus, singing, "Holy, Holy, Holy" (Heb. 10:19–25; 12:22–24). Neither our materiality nor our creaturehood is annihilated. Rather, through this gathering within old creation, we participate in new creation as the Spirit of God takes us into the throne room of God where the heavenly Jerusalem is gathered, just as John was lifted there "in the Spirit" (Rev. 4–5).

The Lord's Supper is more than bread and wine. It is not a regular meal. We may experience God through any meal, whether it is the nightly family meal, the church potluck, or an annual Thanksgiving dinner. Old creation is still good and still mediates God's joyful presence. But the Lord's Supper is more.

The Lord's Supper is the experience of new creation. The bread and wine of the old creation become means through which we experience the new. It is still bread and wine—created materiality is not annihilated—but it also participates in the reality of the new creation through the presence of Christ. Whether we think of that presence in the bread, through the bread, or at the table is inconsequential to this point. The Eucharistic meal is a new creation meal. Rather than annihilating creation, it transforms it, liberates it, and brings it to its goal. In the supper, the living Christ nourishes us. We are nourished by the life of the new creation.

Baptism, the Lord's Supper, and Assembly are sacred moments. They are moments, by the promise of God, where God meets us in this old, frustrated creation so that we might experience—taste and get a glimpse of—new creation. They are moments of authentic participation in the new creation as well as anticipations of its coming fullness. Through the sacraments, God communes with us and confirms our hope. One day the frustrations of creation will pass away, and all creation will be liberated and renewed.

We must have the eyes of faith to see it and experience it. God is present even when we don't realize it. By faith we embrace these sacred moments and lean into the future. By faith we experience grace through Baptism, are nourished at the table, and gather as new humanity around the throne of God.

CONCLUSION

We love the sacraments because they are God's gifts through which we experience new creation and anticipate the new heaven and new earth. They are injections of hope in a broken world, previews of coming attractions, and proleptic experiences of what is to come. Old creation is good, but new creation is better.

BULLET POINTS

- The language of "sacrament" reorients our thinking away from individualistic human-centeredness to communal God-centeredness.
- Sacrament mediates the grace and reality of new creation through the materiality of the present creation.
- Creation is good, but new creation is better.

QUESTIONS

1. Why do many prefer the term *ordinance* in the place of the term *sacrament*? What are the pros/cons or irrelevancy/relevancy of such a discussion?

2. How does asking, "What does God do in this?" rather than, "What do we do in this?" reorient our thinking about Baptism, the Lord's Supper, and Assembly?

3. How have you experienced "new creation" in the sacraments? What are some meaningful experiences in your
   life where your story intersected with God's sacramental
   story?

CHAPTER TWELVE

The Most Ancient Order

Proper Stewardship of God's Creation

*Individual thinkers since the days of Ezekiel
and Isaiah have asserted that the despoliation of
land is not only inexpedient but wrong. Society,
however, has not yet affirmed their belief.*

—Aldo Leopold[1]

*Is it not enough for you to feed on the good pasture,
but you must tread down with your feet the rest of your
pasture? When you drink of clear water, must you foul
the rest with your feet? And must my sheep eat what
you have trodden with your feet, and drink what
you have fouled with your feet?*

—Ezekiel 34:18–19

Do you remember a soul-stirring moment of awe while admiring spectacularly colored autumn leaves framed in a cobalt blue sky? Have you heard someone speak about "having a religious experience" while standing on a mountain summit, astounded by the majesty of phenomenal vistas spread before them? Does the intricacy displayed in a dew-coated spider web cause you to marvel at how God has endowed lowly creatures with astonishing capabilities? Why do camp settings seem so conducive to spiritual revival? Why are our souls aroused by the myriads of stars in the heavens, the sounds of the night, the cool mornings, fresh air, hiking, and swimming in the lake?

The wonders of the natural world evoke inherent awe in people. We seem "wired" with innate reverence for the astounding creation around us. Scripture provides a basis for such feelings. They mirror God's own satisfaction with the primordial handiwork. God's "very good" (Gen. 1:31) seems inscribed in our hearts. Humans, bearing the image of God, innately sense a reverent connection to what God has created, and God's majestic handiwork reveals the author of the universe to our spirits.

How Should We Think about Creation?

Creation is currently experiencing a wide variety of ecological distress, including unprecedentedly rapid loss of numbers and diversity of species; deforestation of formerly verdant landscapes; depletion of oceanic fishery resources; the destruction of native ecosystems through the introduction of harmful exotic plants, animals, and diseases—and the list could go on. While all of us are apprehensively aware of such harm in the world today, we have been reluctant to speak out about pervasive environmental abuse. Christians often seem only vaguely aware and reluctant to fully embrace the vocation for which we were created (Gen. 1:26–28).

Some of the reluctance may arise from fear of ridicule by peers for buying into a perceived "liberal" political ideology. In the late twentieth and the early twenty-first centuries, Christian expressions of concern for pervasive ecological harm were tantamount to blasphemy in some conservative, evangelical Christian circles.

Judeo-Christian values themselves are sometimes identified as the underlying cause of environmental degradation.[2]

Several years ago, while a theology graduate student, I (Mark) was astonished to discover President Jimmy Carter's description of his boyhood experience: "At least one Sunday each year was devoted to protection of the environment, or stewardship of the earth. My father and the other farmers in the congregation would pay close attention to the pastor's sermons, based on texts such as 'The earth is the Lord's, and the fullness thereof (Psalms 24).' When humans were given dominion over the land, water, fish, animals, and all of nature, the emphasis was on careful management and enhancement, not waste or degradation."[3]

The creation care preaching that President Carter remembers occurred in a Southern Baptist church more than eighty years ago. Maybe we should ask ourselves why this important topic, which has only grown more urgent, is still largely absent from many preaching repertoires?

At about the same time Jimmy Carter was listening to annual sermons on creation care (mid-1930s), Aldo Leopold, America's father of ecology, penned a few essays on conservation now compiled in *A Sand County Almanac*. One profound essay, "The Land Ethic," discussed the absence of social conscience relative to good conservation practices. It included this indictment: "No important change in ethics was ever accomplished without an internal change in our intellectual emphasis, loyalties, affections, and convictions. The proof that conservation has not yet touched these foundations of conduct lies in the fact that philosophy and *religion have not yet heard of it*."[4]

Leopold's indictment of religion as partially responsible for apathy toward conservation ethics raises questions: Does inattention to creation care partly result from underdeveloped Christian conviction? Is Bible teaching failing to generate convictions commensurate with the gravity of the inaugural task God ascribed to humanity? Should Christianity involve itself in the realm of environmental protection, or is appealing to faith merely a subversive way to legitimize yet another activist, sociopolitical cause?

Consider God's mandate:

> *Then God said, "Let us make humankind in our image, according to our likeness; and let them have dominion over the fish of the sea, and over the birds of the air and over the cattle, and over the wild animals of the earth, and over every creeping thing that creeps on the earth." (Gen. 1:26)*

In the light of this text, we cannot be indifferent to destructive or environmentally exploitive activities. Much of the secular world believes Christians are apathetic to creation care because churches often fail to champion environmental causes with the ardor devoted to other moral issues.

Reluctance to Embrace Environmental Ethics

Christians generally fall within one of two overarching creation care outlooks. One fosters a strident "subdue [read *use*] the earth" mentality, which often translates into abusive exploitation of the natural world and reduces public support for environmental protection. The other warmly embraces the divine "serve and protect" directive (Gen. 2:15), promoting benevolent protection of the earth's resources and natural beauty.[5] Though Scripture compellingly teaches that humanity is accountable for improper care of creation, those seemingly most familiar with Scripture are often among the most vocal opponents of measures to protect the resources of the earth or foster creation stewardship ethics.

In separate studies correlating the American public's Christian beliefs with their attitudes and behaviors about the environment, a "fundamentalist" mentality was the best predictor for lack of support for protecting the environment.[6] This inverse relationship between fundamentalism and support for creation care ethics is rooted in suspicion toward "environmentalism" as political and moral liberalism: "It is about a focus on this earth rather than heaven, on the universal rather than the national or individual; and about an understanding of what is important that is remote from fundamentalist readings of the Bible. The gaps are very large, and they are exaggerated by the fact that most of the public ecological movement comes dressed in secular or non-Christian clothes. No wonder that for some fundamentalist critics, modern environmentalism is really just another expression of 'secular humanism.'"[7]

A survey by the Pew Research Center on Religion and Public Life shows solid majorities of all major religious groups back stronger measures to protect the environment. However, conservative evangelicals are more reluctant than other groups to make environmental protection a priority.

Further, religion has notably less influence on opinions about environmental policy than other factors do. Only 6 percent said their religious beliefs were the largest influence on their views about protecting the environment. Education and media are the primary drivers of environmental regulations.[8]

Some Christians, already suspicious of science or holding an "it's all going to burn up anyway" attitude, are especially wary of environmental causes due to presumed associations with big government, kooky religions (earth worship), and left-wing ideas.

Richard Cizik, former governmental affairs vice president for the National Association of Evangelicals, describes conservatively oriented, evangelical Christians: "Environmentalism has a sort of a 'left-wing tilt' in their minds. And they haven't had pastors who preached on the importance of creation care. *Most have not had one sermon in their entire biblical life on this topic*, if you can believe that."[9]

Another important reason creation care is an unrecognized priority among some Christians is because most pertinent texts are located in the Hebrew Scriptures. But even if many creation care texts appear in the Hebrew Scriptures, the resulting ethic—rooted in the account of creation—transcends whatever discontinuity one might imagine between the Old and New Testaments. As noted previously in this book, creation care ethics are among the most persistent continuities linking the two testaments.

Some Christians also endorse a pessimistic eschatological outlook, which is especially detrimental to forming a creation stewardship ethic. Dispensational premillennialism is a futuristic perspective often involving a heavenly, apocalyptic war with evil prior to the destruction of the earth. Sensationally promoted by Hal Lindsey's *The Late Great Planet Earth*,[10] Tim Lahaye and Jerry Jenkins's *Left Behind* series,[11] and Christian media, this dooms-day perspective frames the world's problems as signals of the end: "So long as evangelicals hold to an eschatology that understands the world to exist under a divinely imposed death sentence, we should expect no major change in their disposition toward the environment or the environmental movement. They will continue to interpret environmental problems as among the first fruits of an imminent expression of divine wrath against 'the late, great, planet Earth.' Invitations to participate in sustained efforts at solving environmental problems will be thought of as futile at best, and as defying God's will at worst."[12]

The Need for Creation Care Ethics

Scripture takes a dim view of stewards who mismanage entrusted possessions based on self-interest. Consider the parable of the wicked tenants:

> A man planted a vineyard, and leased it to tenants, and went to another country for a long time. When the season came, he sent a slave to the tenants in order that they might give him his share of the produce of the vineyard; but the tenants beat him and sent him away empty-handed. Next he sent another slave; that one also they beat and insulted and sent away empty-handed. And he sent still a third; this one also they wounded and threw out. Then the owner of the vineyard said, 'What shall I do? I will send my beloved son; perhaps they will respect him.' But when the tenants saw him, they discussed it among themselves and said, 'This is the heir; let us kill him so that the inheritance may be ours.' So they threw him out of the vineyard and killed him. What then will the owner of the vineyard do to them? He will come and destroy those tenants and give the vineyard to others. (Luke 20:9–16)

Read this story through the lens of God as the landowner, the vineyard representing the earth and its resources, and humanity as servants entrusted to responsibly care for valuable property they do not own. What outcome is forecast for servants who fail to acknowledge God as the rightful owner of the earth and then add injury to the insult by plundering and despoiling it? If we abusively exploit God's creation for the sake of our own self-interest, we will not escape final accountability. Consider John's warning: "Your wrath has come, and the time for judging the dead, for rewarding Your servants, the prophets and the saints and who fear Your name, both small and great, and *for destroying those who destroy the earth*" (Rev. 11:18; emphasis ours).

As God rules over us, we expect goodness and fairness and for God to continually do what is in humanity's best interests. Therefore, if we count upon God's benevolent rule, why would we ever presume God would approve humanity's abusive, self-serving reign over creation? Exploitive misuse (Ezek. 34:18–19) and wastefulness (John 6:12) are unseemly in God's eyes.

Genesis 9:12–13 testifies to God's love and faithfulness toward creation, which God expects humanity to share: "*This is the sign of the covenant that I make between Me and you and every living creature that is with you*, for all future generations: I have set my bow in the clouds, and it shall be a sign of the covenant between Me and the earth" (Gen. 9:12–13; emphasis ours). God has covenanted with the earth and its life. Consequently, humans, formed in his likeness, must exercise responsible care in ruling what clearly belongs to God.

Wherever I teach creation stewardship, some thank me for articulating what they have always felt in their hearts but did not know how to express. Most people instinctively care about the natural world, but they are unable to conscionably actualize their innate feelings of responsibility toward nature or verbalize what stewardship means. This is the essence of Leopold's criticism of religion's culpability for a substandard conservation ethic in the United States. Our churches, normally involved in the cultivation of societal morals, are often remiss in promoting proper care for the natural world.

Christians value and love creation because God loves it and intends to redeem it alongside humanity. Those who describe God as only caring about humanity are not describing the God revealed in Scripture. The earth and its resources were created by God and declared valuable ("very good") independent of human utility.

Deuteronomy 22:6–7 is one of my favorite biblical texts advocating creation care:

> *If you come on a bird's nest, in any tree or on the ground, with fledglings or eggs, with the mother sitting on the fledglings or on the eggs, you shall not take the mother with the young. Let the mother go, taking only the young for yourself, in order that it may go well with you and you may live long.*

When I took my first wildlife management class in college, the professor said something astonishing that I had never heard before. This Deuteronomic prescription is the oldest known written law about wildlife conservation. In effect, God charged ancient Israel with game warden responsibilities.

And there are other examples. In Exodus it says, "But the seventh year you shall let [the crop field] rest and lie fallow, so that the poor of your people may eat; and what they leave the wild animals may eat. You shall do the same with your vineyard, and with your olive orchard" (23:11). In Leviticus it says, "When you reap the harvest of your land, you shall not reap to the very edges of your field, or gather the gleanings of your harvest" (19:9).

Conservation practices—mandated in the Torah—benefited land, people, and wildlife. We have similar agricultural programs in the United States, which pay farmers to leave portions of their crop fields unplanted (fallow) or unharvested to increase soil fertility and to provide food and cover for wildlife. In another passage, God expects those who prosecute wars to protect trees:

> *If you besiege a town for a long time, making war against it in order to take it, you must not destroy its trees by wielding an ax against them. Although you may take food from them, you must not cut them down. Are trees in the field human beings that they should come under siege from you? (Deut. 20:19)*

If ancient warriors were responsible for executing their plans in a conservationist manner, there is little doubt what God might think about modern technological warfare whose collateral damage often results in widespread despoliation of the land.

CONCLUSION

Western Christianity appears poised to restore insights about creation and a first-century eschatological outlook free from Gnostic dualism. "Heaven" as an ethereal home beyond the skies is actually incongruent with biblical expectations and hope. Scripture never says heaven, separated from the earth, is the eternal destiny of the redeemed. Forecasting a doomed earth and an eternal celestial abode can result in an escapist outlook that hunkers down until we "fly away," diminishing support for creation stewardship. The true biblical hope is for a fiery refinement of every aberrant aspect of "fallen creation" and a triumphant, redemptive reclamation of everything God pronounced "very good" (Gen. 1:31).

Let us be faithful to our instinctive reverence for God's creation and Scripture's call to responsibly care for the resources of the earth. In all aspects of our lives, let us promote proper reverence for what belongs to God.

BULLET POINTS

- Humans were formed in God's image to serve as curators of God's creation, whose vastness, beauty, and intricacy bear witness to God.
- Cultural and religious misconceptions generate reluctance to teach and practice creation care ethics.
- God will hold humanity accountable for self-centered abuse and detrimental mismanagement of God's creation.

QUESTIONS

1. What within creation evokes awe and beauty in you? What place in creation gives you peace and rest?

2. Does your church promote creation care? If so, in what way?

3. Which unsustainable, exploitive environmental practice(s) (e.g., overfishing, species extinction, loss of rainforest, converting farmland to other uses, etc.) most concern you? What can we do to address these problems?

CHAPTER THIRTEEN

Exemplary Creation Stewardship

*A thing is right when it tends to preserve the
integrity, stability and beauty of the biotic
community. It is wrong when it tends otherwise.*

—Aldo Leopold[1]

*Many of the world's coral reefs are already barren
or in a state of constant decline. "Who turned
the wonderworld of the seas into underwater
cemeteries bereft of colour and life?"*

—Pope Francis[2]

Almost daily, we are bombarded by images of rivers turned orange by leaking mine effluent and ocean beaches littered with medical waste. We also hear stories about mercury-contaminated fish, disappearing rainforests and coral reefs, and the rapid extinction of many forms of life. We even face the possibility that pollution from heavy use of fossil fuels may lead to harmful increases in the temperature of our planet. Our worry and frustration brings to mind the old joke, "If we were renting the earth from God, our landlord would keep our damage deposit!"

Finding Our Voice for Creation Care Responsibility

I (Mark) worked in the field of ecological protection for thirty-five years and attended many public hearings focused on controversial conservation issues (try explaining to sheep ranchers why they should embrace reintroducing grizzly bears and wolves into western ecosystems!). The testimony and presentations I heard over the years were always appeals to regulatory and political authorities to respect "the God-given rights" of various individuals and groups, claiming they might be adversely affected by natural resource management decisions. Sadly, not once did I ever see a church group or religious representative remind such audiences of their "God-given responsibility" to act as conscionable stewards, expected to rule wisely over what is entrusted to our care.

What might happen if we appealed to the divine mandates in Scripture, in addition to the usual reasons (health, economics, etc.) ordinarily put forth, to advocate proper care of the earth and its resources? In 2005, I attended a fish conservation symposium in Jackson, Montana. Though I was not representing a government conservation agency, I gave a presentation about the conservation of rare fish species. My presentation included a theological rationale in addition to other reasons typically offered to justify protecting rare species. Many were surprised, some squirmed in their seats, and others glared in disbelief. Folks were unprepared to discuss religious reasons for ecological stewardship, although afterward, several thanked me for articulating a theological rationale.

Late in the evening, when the crowd had thinned out, the governor's chief of staff summoned me into a quiet corner. I expected admonishment for "stepping out of bounds" because I appealed to theology to spur conservation efforts. To my surprise (and relief), he expressed his personal gratitude for reminding everyone about Scripture's legitimization of conservation. When he was a boy, he said, his father often used their fishing and camping trips to instruct him about Christian responsibility for wise stewardship of Montana's wondrous natural resources. This illustrates how people often appreciate hearing God's advocacy for creation care.

Environmental problems do not merely depict human failings to execute our primordial job description; they attest to the condition of our relationship to God. Hosea 4:1–3 describes how the earth's resources act as a kind of barometer of the health for humanity's relationship to God. Christian theology challenges ecologically avaricious consumerism and gluttonous self-centered lifestyles. We learn to worship the Lord of all creation by finding joy in the quality rather than the quantity of our possessions.

Meaningful Creation Care Suggestions

Christians frequently take action on a variety of moral issues across the board. However, many are unsure how to help protect God's creation. How do we modify our lifestyles, individually and collectively, and change our attitudes and practices to keep the Genesis mandate? How do we live as exemplary stewards of creation?

There is not enough space to provide detailed scientific analyses or to recommend ways to solve the earth's plethora of ecological problems. However, the suggested resources section located at the end of this book lists several articles and books for further reading on the topic of Christian environmental stewardship and how to more effectively care for creation. Several websites are listed for estimating the environmental impact (or carbon footprint) we have on the earth. Running a quick calculation takes only a few minutes, and the results may surprise you. Local libraries also provide access to many resources (books, journals, magazines, and videos) devoted to ecological problems and remedies, including lowering our carbon footprint, living sustainably, and suggesting ways to "green up" our lifestyles. Following the outline of Genesis 1:26–28, here are a few practical suggestions for meaningful creation care action.

The Fish of the Sea

The oceans cover two-thirds of the earth, producing half of the world's oxygen, regulating our climate, and providing approximately one billion people with their primary source of protein. It is difficult to comprehend how human activity might irreparably damage such a vast area, but it is happening. Overfishing, regulatory difficulties, and our consumption habits all contribute to precipitous declines in wild fish. Nearly two-thirds of assessed oceanic fish populations are unhealthy, and the unassessed are probably in worse shape.[3] The following are some examples:

1. Once a staple of the North Atlantic fishing economy, the cod fishery completely collapsed in the early 1990s and has shown little evidence of recovery two decades later.
2. The breeding population of Pacific bluefin tuna is now at only about 4 percent of its original size.
3. Coral reefs, home to a quarter of the ocean's fish, are declining at an alarming rate.
4. An area known as the "Great Pacific Garbage Patch" contains plastic rubbish and debris, covering an area similar in size to Texas.

However, much can be done. We can purchase and eat seafood "sustainably." According to the National Oceanic and Atmospheric

Administration (NOAA), sustainability is based on a simple principle—meeting today's needs without compromising the ability of future generations to meet theirs.[4] This means catching or farming seafood responsibly with consideration for the long-term health of the environment and the livelihoods of people who depend on it.

What really matters is to only purchase finfish and shellfish caught or farmed through ecologically responsible techniques. The experts at Seafood Watch[5] have done the work for us. They provide consumer guides, which indicate the best choices of seafood so ocean fisheries might recover and remain healthy. They also have downloadable, state-by-state fish consumption guidelines and a smartphone app so we will always have ready access to this information. The brochures are suitable for distribution in a church Bible class, state fair booths, use in small group discussions, or for retreat-setting discussions. Let's encourage our favorite seafood shop, grocery store, and restaurants to follow these guidelines. This uses market forces to promote ethical, sustainable fishing practices, which lead to healthier populations of fish and sea life.

The Birds of the Air

When Europeans began exploring North America, ornithologists estimate there were three to five billion passenger pigeons, comprising 25 to 40 percent of the total North American bird population. Their numbers darkened the sky each spring as they migrated from the South to the Midwest, and again on their return journey in the fall. Clearing huge swaths of forest and overhunting led to their extinction. Martha, the last remaining passenger pigeon, died at the Cincinnati Zoological Garden on September 1, 1914.

One hundred years after the extinction of the passenger pigeon, the nation's top bird science and conservation groups came together and published "The State of the Birds 2014," the most comprehensive review of long-term trend data for US birds ever conducted.[6] The unsettling report shows bird populations generally declining across several key habitats, and it includes a "watch list" of bird species in need of immediate conservation assistance. For example, back from the brink of extinction, our nation's symbol, the bald eagle, is off the endangered species list and doing well. But other formerly common and popular species, such as the eastern meadowlark, northern bobwhite quail, and bobolink, are declining steeply across their range. More than half of all native shorebird species are on the watch list, and Hawaii's native birds comprise one-third of all the birds on the US endangered species list.

What can we do to meaningfully help birds? One significant way to support bird habitat conservation is to purchase, at the local post office, a federal duck stamp, which is among the most successful conservation tools ever created to protect habitat for birds and other wildlife. Ninety-eight percent of the purchase price goes directly to help acquire and protect wetland habitat conservation easements for the US National Wildlife Refuge System. Wetlands (and surrounding grasslands for nesting) acquired with duck stamp dollars are some of the most biologically productive ecosystems on earth. These areas help purify water; aid in flood control; reduce soil erosion; provide food, shelter, and nesting habitat for a huge variety of birds; and facilitate multiple forms of outdoor recreation.[7]

We may also help birds by participating in an annual Christmas Bird Count (CBC). All CBCs are conducted each year between December 14 and January 5. Each CBC takes place in an established fifteen-mile-diameter circle and is organized by a count compiler. CBC volunteers follow specified routes within the designated circle, counting every bird they see or hear all day. This is not merely a species tally—the volunteers count all birds seen, providing an estimate of the total number of birds within the circle that day. The data from all census areas across the country are then compiled and used as indices of the health of wild bird populations in the United States. Anyone can participate. Beginners join a group of experienced birdwatchers. Because of the need to adhere to a systematic method for conducting the CBC, participants should make advanced arrangements with the circle compiler. The Audubon Society has all necessary details.

Cattle

"Cattle" probably envisions all livestock (beef, pork, poultry, etc.). The media has increased coverage of inhumane animal husbandry practices. We have seen photos of chickens or pigs crammed into tight cages, force-fed, and pumped full of antibiotics and hormones, and cattle in feedlots wallowing in their own excrement. Some remedies to these situations are still developing. For now, we can purchase meat, eggs, and dairy products from producers who treat their livestock as humanely as possible. When making such purchases at a grocery store, look for a Certified Humane[8] or a similar type of packaging label. This rewards ethical producers and creates economic demand for more responsible practices.

In the near term, there is usually some extra expense associated with purchasing meat, eggs, and dairy products from humane animal husbandry producers, and this recommendation might be difficult for many. Attempts to live a lifestyle providing conscionable witness to creation care's importance may come with some increased costs, and we may count it as part of the cost of discipleship as we live out God's love story with creation (Luke 14:27–28).

The Wild Animals of the Earth

Because the need for wildlife conservation is so large and varies from place to place, the most helpful thing to recommend is education. The United States has an internationally unique system of nearly six hundred national wildlife refuges, comprising more than one hundred fifty million acres.[9] We recommend taking a scout troop, youth group, small group, or Bible class to visit one. You can arrange your trip at times when wildlife viewing is at its peak and when a biologist can guide your group. Some people may become sufficiently interested to serve as refuge volunteers and assist with various conservation activities conducted there.

State wildlife management agencies can assist churches and homeowners in creating wildlife habitat, even in urban areas. Many have urban wildlife managers, and they can advise your scout troops, small groups, and individual church members about creating church campus and backyard wildlife habitat demonstration areas. We can erect bird and bat houses, plant flowers attractive to hummingbirds and pollinator insects, provide water features helpful to frogs and turtles, set out bird and squirrel feeders, and many other things to help wildlife specific to an area.

Also, some churches decorate their buildings with a creation theme characteristic of their area of the country. They commission a pulpit backdrop, use lots of plants and greenery, and even pipe in ambient outdoor (forest, ocean, etc.) sounds into the church entryway and auditoriums at appropriate times.

Every Living Thing That Moves upon the Earth

Only about 15 percent of all species on earth have been discovered. Sadly, many have gone extinct before they were cataloged. One beloved (and highly visible) species, the monarch butterfly, is especially representative of the current rapid decline of many species around the world. Millions of monarchs spend November through March hibernating in a very small patch of temperate forest in Mexico after a journey of nearly twenty-five hundred miles across North America. But in the span of only twenty years, the wintering area has shrunk from about fifty acres to less than two, and one of nature's greatest migration spectacles might vanish forever.

One large factor in the decline of monarch populations is the reduction of milkweed caused by crop-related herbicides. In response, we can plant milkweed (which has a beautiful flower), the primary food source for monarch larvae, around our gardens, in suitable areas of our church campuses, or any idle space. We can work with our local nurseries or native plant dealers and establish plots of milkweed for the butterflies to colonize. We can also obtain free milkweed seeds, monarch conservation advice, and even order caterpillars to place in planted milkweed patches or raise in screened cages.[10] These are wonderful activities for children and adult Christians interested in caring for creation.

By engaging in monarch butterfly conservation, people will learn a great deal about wildlife migration, species interactions, insect population dynamics, and maybe even find a useful metaphor or two for theological discussion (resurrection, baptism, transformation, etc.).

Five More Considerations for "Greener" Churches and Congregants

Energy. Do an energy audit of churches and homes. Utility companies suggest ways (e.g., wrapping your water heater, caulking windows, using weather strip doors) to cut your energy bill and save money. Also, install programmable thermostats in your churches and homes to save energy at night and when unoccupied.

Light. Illumination has been revolutionized by energy-efficient light emitting diode (LED) and compact fluorescent lights (CFL). Install them inside and outside churches and homes to save energy and money. Again, we recognize this may increase household expenses, but the energy savings may offset such costs.

Paper. Recycle paper. Purchase recycled paper for church and home printers, and put a box beside them to collect waste paper to take to your local recycling facility.

Drink. If you drink coffee or serve it at church, use shade-grown beans or grounds to protect neotropical migratory bird (e.g., scarlet tanagers, Baltimore orioles) wintering areas in Central and South America. Look for "bird friendly"[11] certification stickers on coffee packages. Use eco-friendly linguine pasta strips for coffee stirrers instead of the "use-once and throw away" plastic sticks. Encourage the use of personal insulated coffee cups instead of discardable paper or Styrofoam cups. Carry a reusable plastic or metal container for water.

Delegate. Consider appointing an interested person to lead the church in creation care and sustainability in the congregation.

CONCLUSION

Observing the earth's ecological problems may leave us feeling sad, overwhelmed, and disheartened. None of us can single-handedly solve these problems. God must do the heavy lifting in healing the earth. Nevertheless, we all must advocate for proper care of God's creation, help where we can, and in so doing serve as witnesses to good stewardship for the earth God loves.

BULLET POINTS

- In contrast to most other moral issues, Christians are often less sure about using Scripture to advocate for the proper care of God's creation.
- The slumping ecological health of the earth reflects humanity's deteriorated relationship with God (Hos. 4:1–3).
- Though the ecological problems of the earth seem insurmountable, there are many helpful practices Christians can implement.

QUESTIONS

1. What biblical or principled appeals have you used to advocate for the proper care of God's creation? What happened?

2. Do you think the ecological health of the earth mimics the quality of humanity's relationship with God? How is this reflected in our world?

3. Which of the suggested conservation activities seem most appealing and practical to you? Why?

CHAPTER FOURTEEN

God's Restoration Movement

Revisioning the Restoration Plea

*Heaven must receive him until the time comes
for God to restore everything as he promised
long ago through his holy prophets.*

—Acts 3:21 (NIV)

Restoration.

That word has inspired generations of disciples in Churches
of Christ. We have produced powerful sermons and literature on
the necessity and urgency of the restoration plea. They are clar-
ion calls for restoring the right name, congregational autonomy,
male leadership, five acts of worship, and the five steps of salvation.
Through restoration, we belong to the one true church.

There is, however, no *one* Stone-Campbell Movement restoration *plea*. This will surprise many unfamiliar with our history.
Rather, there are Stone-Campbell Movement restoration *pleas*.
Nevertheless, though Barton Stone, Thomas and Alexander Campbell, and Walter Scott had significantly different understandings

on many identity markers, two impulses bound them together: a deep aversion to the chaotic state of Christian division on the US frontier and a profound sense of purpose driven by eschatology.

Deeply convinced God was moving in contemporary world events—like the American Revolution and the Great Awakening—to bring history to its goal, they called Christians to abandon divisive postures. Because the millennium was in sight, disciples did not have the luxury of an internecine war among themselves.

The problem was disunity, and this subverted God's goal. Consequently, Christians had to find ways to come together, responding to Jesus's high priestly prayer (John 17:20–26). In the interest of unity, Alexander Campbell wrote a lengthy series of thirty-two articles in *The Christian Baptist* (1826–27) called "A Restoration of the Ancient Order of Things." This outlined the ancient order as Alexander understood it, but he did not make it a test of communion. The only tests of fellowship for Alexander were faith in Jesus and Christian obedience. He is quite explicit that the "ancient order" is not about fellowship. It was a tool by which Christians might come together as a visible, united community by conforming to the order found in Scripture.[1] Because Stone, the Campbells, and Scott were focused on the eschatological quest for the unity of the church, when others turned the question into a search for the one true church, they resisted it. Eventually, Campbell's restoration order was turned into something else and was no longer a proposal to fulfill Christ's unity prayer. It became a means of evangelism where all others were excluded from the Christian church if they did not follow the exact order Campbell had identified. The order became a test of communion, and this subverted the original vision for the movement.

By the twentieth century, the profound eschatological frame holding together a diverse Stone-Campbell Movement had degenerated into debates about the interpretation of predictive prophecy and the meaning of Revelation 20. Eventually, when Churches of Christ lost this earlier eschatological consciousness, ecclesiology in the form of the marks of the true church was what remained.

While Alexander Campbell's own vision stressed the covenantal, narrative nature of biblical theology, his ecclesial hermeneutic was co-opted to deal with "church questions" and set the boundaries of fellowship. This hermeneutic posited the New Testament as the church's *law book*. The New Testament, particularly Acts 2 through Jude, became a uniform pattern describing the golden age of the church. The pattern of restoration, from this perspective, lies in the past.

Restoration from Another Direction

We gladly affirm the historic position of the Stone-Campbell Movement on the Bible as the supreme authority for faith and practice. While we claim all the treasures of sanctified wisdom from the saints of the past, Scripture alone retains our ultimate allegiance. We also affirm Campbell's emphasis on the biblical narrative as a whole, and this provides a way to understand restoration more faithfully. There are remarkable similarities between Campbell's approach and contemporary interpreters like N. T. Wright.[2]

The Bible tells the story of the kingdom of God. Scripture moves toward the achievement of God's purposes for the whole of creation. To have eyes to see what God is doing requires a hermeneutic shaped by the canon itself. In other words, our canonical hermeneutic is narrative in form. The "metanarrative" interprets the world for us and provides the tools to live faithfully as God's people in the present.

In the biblical canon, the "plot" of God's story is easily recognized. Large blocks of material in the Bible narrate the story.

Genesis to Second Kings (minus Ruth) tells a single integrated story from creation to the fall of Jerusalem. Chronicles and Ezra through Nehemiah *retell the same story*, updating details after the Exile. Along the way there are "asides," which summarize or highlight the most significant parts of the story (e.g., Deut. 1–4; Josh. 24:1–15; Judg. 11:15–28; 1 Sam. 12; Neh. 9). Each retelling occurs at a critical juncture. God's people remember their identity, their mission, and are renewed. These retellings point God's people to the future. They do not restore the past; they are restoring the future. The future, in a sense, depends on God's people becoming what God placed them in the world to become.

In the plot, the Creator is identified as the God of Abraham, Isaac, and Jacob, which is the first step in becoming the God of all people and Lord of all creation. God, God's people, and God's world are related to each other in every stage of the narrative even though each telling is not identical. The story "moves on," but the characters and mission remain the same.

Put another way, when we move into the New Testament writings, the characters are the same. The story of the church does not replace the one in the Hebrew Bible. The story of the church is the continuation of the same people of God. The church is the place where God's promises of blessing, redemption, and new creation have broken into the old lamenting creation to establish a beachhead as God's renewed and resurrected Israel.

According to the story, the goal of restoration is not an attempt to return to any historical golden age. It is not the age of Abraham, David, or Nehemiah. God enabled Israel, flawed as they were, to function by God's grace in their present. The story was their map and their clock. As God's people, they were no longer in the same place, and clearly they were not at the same time. The story did not foster faithfulness to a distant past but openness to God's future. The plot points to the future. Living it faithfully restores not the past but the future.

What is this future within the biblical story? Campbell knew it as the "creation of a new universe, new heavens, new earth, all things new."[3] That is the goal of the story. We are faithful to the story when we restore the future. We live the resurrection life even now; we embody the life of the future in the present. In other words, as disciples of the one who died and was raised as the first fruit of God's new creation, we practice the future.

Restoring God's World to God's Rule

In a sermon remarkably like the periodic summaries of the Bible noted above, Peter assures his audience God is faithful to the promises. Though they killed the "Author of life," God raised him from the dead. Repentance is the faithful response, which results in "times of refreshing" coming from the "presence of the Lord." While we are given time for repentance, Peter informs us, the raised Messiah "must remain in heaven until the time of universal restoration that God announced long ago through the prophets" (Acts 3:15, 19–21). The gospel of Jesus began with the promises to the Patriarchs. Peter's sermon follows a crippled beggar's restoration to health—a Jubilee moment—and climaxes with God's restoration movement.

The gospel in Acts 3 is not merely the good news of personal salvation. God mercifully keeps Jesus in heaven to provide seasons where people may respond to the gospel. But the sermon, the story, is eschatological. Jesus "must" remain in heaven "until" the time of promised "universal restoration." The gospel is the culmination of the story where "all things" are restored (Acts 3:21 NIV). Peter reveals the goal of the story—God's redemptive purposes for creation are seen in the healing of a cripple who typifies the restoration of the world to God's rule. The goal of salvation is God's restoration movement.

Paul opens his letter to the Ephesians with a splendid prayer of praise. It reveals the profound "mystery" of God's "plan" of salvation. God's purpose in redemption, the lavishing of his inexhaustible grace, is cosmic. God unveils the mystery, and the word *mystery* does not refer to something unknown. Rather, it means something like having the inside scoop on God's plan. The revealed mystery—the open secret—is "to gather up all things in him, things in heaven and things on earth" (Eph. 1:10).

God's restoration movement unites the two halves of God's world: heaven and earth. In the person of Christ, God will heal the cosmic division within creation. Heaven and earth were one in the beginning but humans vandalized it. In Jesus, who unites God and creation through incarnation, heaven and earth are joined together forever. They are restored. Indeed, they are more than restored in Christ; the whole cosmos is transformed into an eternal home where God will dwell with humanity.

God's restoration movement does not take us back to the first century; it moves us into the future. It restores creation so the will of God is done on earth as it is in heaven (Matt. 6:10). God's people participate in God's restoration as they practice resurrection by letting the future guide them in the present. Indeed, as royal priests, we proclaim the "mighty acts" of God who showers grace, restores *shalom*, and unites creation in Jesus the Messiah by the power of the Spirit.

Restoring God's *Shalom* to Fractured Humanity

As we have seen, God chose Abraham and the land as representative of all humanity and the world. Israel is placed in the world, like leaven, as God's healing blessing to the nations.

Yet humanity tends to war with God, with each other, and with creation. Violence in all its manifestations—from the battle of the sexes to unbridled destruction of God's animals—is the polar opposite of *shalom*. God's salvation tears down the walls of hostility, real or imagined, that humans erect.

God placed Israel in the world to display God's future. Sadly, like God's people today, Israel often reflected the image of the evil one rather than the image of God. Just as Adam before them, Israel vandalized God's Eden, the land into which God had brought them. But the prophets repeatedly dream of a new Eden and the wonder of its *shalom*. Micah, for example, longs for a day when justice is established and the nations will stream to Israel to learn the way of the Lord. In God's land, through Israel, God teaches the nations to learn war no more and to destroy their weapons of war. Instead of war, they will sit among the trees feasting on the fruit of the land because they are no longer "afraid" (Mic. 4:1–4).

Isaiah, echoing Genesis 12:3, envisioned a time when God's people would be "a blessing in the midst of the earth." The ancient enemies of God's people—Egypt, the enemy of her enslavement, and Assyria, the destroyer of the northern kingdom—are blessed because God's people are in the world. This blessing is the death of enmity: "On that day Israel will be the third with Egypt and Assyria, a blessing in the midst of the earth, whom the LORD of hosts has blessed, saying, 'Blessed be Egypt my people, and Assyria the work of my hands, and Israel my heritage'" (Isa. 19:24–25). When Israel lives in creation as God intended, even the Egyptians and Assyrians know the Lord and worship the God of Israel.

The New Testament identifies God's church as the place where the future becomes a reality. The vision of Egyptians, Assyrians, and Israelites sitting together at the table of *shalom* is the symbol of God's restoration movement. If God has made heaven and earth "one" through the "Christ Event," then the goal of the story is realized—the ancient fracturing of the human family is healed through Israel's Messiah:

> *Scripture foresaw that God would justify the Gentiles by faith, and announced the gospel in advance to Abraham: "All nations will be blessed through you." So those who rely on faith are blessed along with Abraham, the man of faith. (Gal. 3:8–9 NIV)*

> *There is neither Jew nor Gentile, neither slave nor free, nor is there male and female, for you are all one in Christ Jesus. If you belong to Christ, then you are Abraham's seed, and heirs according to the promise. (Gal. 3:28–29 NIV)*

> *But now in Christ Jesus you who were once far off have been brought near by the blood of Christ. For he is our peace; in his flesh he has made both groups into one and has broken down the dividing wall, that is the hostility between us.*
> *(Eph. 2:13–14 NRSV)*

God's restoration movement is nothing less than the re-creation of the human race, which transcends the categories of least and greatest. Restored Israel—the church—is a new race that belongs to the future (1 Peter 2:9), though she lives in the present as an exile and alien. She embodies the *shalom* of Eden glorified in Christ.

The church, as God's new creation, exhibits the diversity of creation itself. Diversity is as good as the "very good" God pronounced over it in Genesis. Paul recognizes this when he calls Jewish and Gentile believers to tolerate their ethnic and religious diversity (Rom. 14). Paul welcomes this diversity for the sake of *shalom* and the oneness of the kingdom. Some people, like Paul, honor the liturgical calendar, while others think it is foolishness. Some embrace vegetarian lifestyles and others eat with no questions asked. Some abstain from any alcohol for various reasons and others sip with joy. Diverse worship practices are not antithetical to oneness in Christ, and no one should judge the other. This rich diversity wells up together as a symphony of praise to the one who has healed the divisions among us (Rom. 15:5–6).

The history of salvation is the history of God's mission to restore creation. To accomplish this, God initiated every movement within the story. Restoration is always about what God has done, is doing, and will do:

> *God sent Abraham,*
> *God sent Israel,*
> *God sent Jesus,*
> *God sent the Spirit, and*
> *God sent renewed Israel, the church,*
> *in order to restore creation to full communion with God.*

God's faithful people know where and when they are in the story. They know the story of God's restoration movement in the past. They know God's purposes in creation, why God called Israel into being, and the goal of the story. We do not live in the past. Remembering the past awakens our minds to God's future. Through God's people, God restores the world's future.

CONCLUSION

The Stone-Campbell Movement appropriately lamented the warfare among disciples of Christ. "Schism in the Christian church" is, Alexander Campbell rightly said, "the capital sin of the age against the Lord's anointed."[4] When we understand God's restoration movement, seeking visible unity is an expression of fidelity to the gospel itself, even as we accept each other as Christ has accepted us (Rom. 15:7).

Restoration in the Bible is the mission of God to heal all, bring everything into communion with God, and to participate in the union of all things in Christ.

BULLET POINTS

- God's restoration movement seeks to unite the two halves of God's good creation in the person of Jesus the Messiah.
- God's restoration movement restores God's future to the world.
- God's restoration movement restores Israel as a new humanity through which new creation breaks into the world.

QUESTIONS

1. Why is it important to understand not only the facts of God's story but also its goal? How does the story illuminate where we are and what time it is?

2. What is the goal of God's restoration movement? What practices embrace God's purposes?

3. Does God's restoration movement enhance or diminish diversity?

Curiosities and Supposed Countertexts

Whenever we talk about the new heaven and the new earth, two kinds of questions consistently arise. One we call "curiosities," and the other identifies supposed "countertexts."

Heaven's Curiosities

What exactly will it be like in the new heaven and new earth? The biblical trajectory does not give us much information. Revelation 21–22 is filled with metaphors and symbols, and even Isaiah 65 presents an idealistic picture of life within the old creation, though it is called "new." Consequently, we must humbly acknowledge there is more we don't know than we do know about our eternal state.

Most of our questions about the particulars are quite speculative. For a few there are potentially helpful answers, but on the whole these speculations miss the point of the biblical story. We do not pursue or think about new creation theology so we might be comforted by the particulars of the eternal state. Rather, we affirm it because it is the trajectory of the story itself, which shapes our vocation and hope. The story is about the defeat of death, the resurrection of the body, and the renewal of heaven and earth as

God's dwelling place. Other than that, the Bible is not too specific about what new creation involves or what it will look like. Perhaps we should be content with the hope of the new heaven and new earth rather than agonizing about its future specifics, which may supplant hope with curiosity.

Nevertheless, our curiosity remains. It is difficult to avoid. So let's consider a few broad questions.

Sexual Identity and Relationships

In the resurrection, Jesus noted, we will be "like the angels" in that there will be no marriage in the new world (Mark 12:25). This is disturbing for many, since it seems like we lose something we value in this life—our marriage partners.

On the one hand, we don't think this means a loss of sexual embodiment. Our resurrection bodies are yet human, and our humanity still reflects the fullness of the divine image through the community of male and female. We will continue to image God as male and female in the new creation.

On the other hand, the relationship of male and female is heightened rather than lost. This does not mean sexual relations will exist. Rather, sexual relations serve the purpose of intimacy and procreation in the old creation. Because the needs of procreation are complete in the new creation (all creation has been filled) and intimacy is experienced in a fuller, richer way, there is no need for sexual relations. Instead, "sex," while presently a dynamic imaging of God's own intimacy, is transcended in the new creation by the nature of the relationship all humans will have with each other. We will experience intimacy with each other in ways we cannot now imagine, except perhaps when our marriages or relationships in small groups give us a taste of that future.

Our human identity continues from the present into the future, and part of that identity is our relationships. We will continue them in the future, and they will deepen throughout eternity. Those relationships will expand as others are included in that intimacy. Our life in the new creation is a dynamic journey into deeper intimacy with others, a journey we can only barely imitate in our deepest relationships in the present (especially our marriages or closest friends as singles).

This includes our relationship with God. New creation does not mean we become omniscient or infinite. God will be new to us every morning as our finite minds continue to learn more about God, who is a bottomless well from which we will continually drink. Our relationship with God is an eternal journey into God's love, and we will never reach a stopping point. We will never exhaust God's resources.

Human Vocation and Culture

The original Garden of Eden will become a new Jerusalem with a garden. In part, the garden is not so much restored as glorified. The new Jerusalem is the goal of God's dynamic activity within creation. The goal is not mere restoration but transformation and glorification. The new creation is better than Eden!

Like Eden, however, humanity has a purpose in the new creation. The new creation is no more static than the original one. Humanity was tasked with developing creation, including enjoying and ordering it. This includes creating human culture.

Human culture will flourish in the new creation, just as it was intended in the old. We will create new literature, art, and music. We will build and enjoy our labors. We will till the soil and enjoy the fruit of the earth in new ways similar to the old. We will play and rest. We will worship. Human culture will progress as we engage the tasks God has given us as corulers and priests within creation. Our role as divine imagers within creation remains in the new world. We will rest with God in the new creation, and this rest includes fully participating in our renewed mission within God's creation.

New Creation Life

Creation will still exist, including animals. When God created, God blessed the animals as well as humans. God delights in them, as do people.

The new creation will exhibit the same kind of diversity of life and terrain it presently exhibits, and we cannot begin to imagine what "glorification" will mean for creation when it is liberated from its bondage to decay. We can speculate, but our imaginations are limited and deeply embedded in the old creation.

Let us trust God with new creation. We cannot dictate it and we cannot imagine it. Given God's love for creation and God's delight in it, the new creation will not be less than the present one. Indeed, we anticipate something much more, beyond our feeble imaginations.

What we do know is this: God will dwell there, we will dwell with God, and God will glorify creation. This is ultimately what is most important.

Countertexts?

Invariably, three biblical texts are quickly on the lips of those who doubt the earth's renewal. Consequently, we briefly comment on each below, and note how each text coheres with this book's perspective.

We also recognize there are other texts and potentially other trajectories that may exist in tension with our reading of Scripture. We hope our approach throughout this book has taken many of those into account, though we could not possibly address every question or concern within this brief work.

John 14:2–3

> *In my Father's house there are many dwelling places. If it were not so, would I have told you that I go to prepare a place for you? And if I go and prepare a place for you, I will come again and will take you to myself, so that where I am, there you may be also.*

Jesus is going away, and he is coming again.

When he comes again, he will receive (*paralambano*) us—that is, take us into his own possession. This contrasts with how Jesus himself was received. He came among his own people, but they did not receive him (John 1:11). Rather than rejecting us, Jesus will dwell with us, just as he came among us to dwell in the flesh (John 1:14)

Where will Jesus dwell with us or receive us? We have two descriptions in the text. First, there are rooms (dwelling places; *monai*) in the Father's house. We will dwell with the Father where God dwells. The "Father's house" is an allusion to the temple of God where God dwells.

In one sense, Jesus comes even now in the presence of the Spirit to live within us and to make his home among us. This is his promise in John 14:23, the only place where Jesus uses this word other than John 14:2. In the coming of the Spirit, the Father and Son, Jesus said, will "make our home [dwelling place] with them."

But Jesus envisions yet a fuller experience of dwelling with God than the indwelling of the Spirit in the present. The time will come when God will dwell with humanity in God's own house or temple.

Second, going away, Jesus is preparing a place (*topon*) for us. The place is God's house, or temple. The Christ Event has prepared a place for us to dwell with God, and even now Jesus continues to "prepare" that place.

What is the "Father's house"? It may refer to the heavenly sanctuary, but it may also refer to the cosmic sanctuary (cf. Isa. 66:1–2). Creation is God's house, and the new creation—the new heaven and new earth—is God's dwelling place (cf. Rev. 21:1–4). Even if we understand it as the heavenly sanctuary, according to Revelation 21, that sanctuary will itself come to the new earth.

Jesus goes away to complete the construction (preparation) of God's new house, the new creation. When Jesus returns, the heavenly Jerusalem will descend—with Jesus—to the new earth under the new heavens. Jesus will receive us, and we will dwell with Jesus within the Father's house forever.

2 Peter 3:6–7, 13

> *By the word of God heavens existed long ago and an earth was formed out of water and by means of water, through which the world at that time was deluged with water and perished. But by the same word the present heavens and earth are reserved for fire, being kept until the day of judgment and the destruction of the godless . . . But, in accordance with his promise, we wait for new heavens and new earth, where righteousness is at home.*

Second Peter 3 envisions three habitable worlds:

1. The original "heavens" and "earth" that emerged from and through water by the command of God (2 Peter 3:5).
2. The "present heavens and earth" that are "reserved for fire" at the command of God (2 Peter 3:7, 10, 12).
3. The future "new heavens and a new earth where righteousness is at home," according to the promise of God (2 Peter 3:13).

The first world was "destroyed" (from *apollumi*) by water, and the second world is destined to "destruction" (*apoleto*) by fire. In the wake of that destruction, a new heaven and earth will appear.

The critical questions are (1) the nature of the destruction as well as (2) the origin and nature of the new heaven and new earth.

The first world was "destroyed" but it was not annihilated. The old world was washed away, but when the waters receded, a new world emerged. Though the cosmos perished, nevertheless it continued to exist and it gave new life. The water not only judges the earth, it also cleanses it as creation is rebirthed through water.

In the same way, the present *heavens* will "pass away" and "dissolve" (or loosed, from *luo*) with the noise of a crackling fire (2 Peter 3:10, 12), the "*elements*" will be "dissolved" (or loosed, *luo*) and "melt" by fire (2 Peter 3:10, 12), and the *earth* with its works will be "disclosed" (found or laid bare; 2 Peter 3:10). When the fire completes its work, a new heaven and new earth will appear (2 Peter 3:13).

What, however, is the function of the fire? Does it annihilate the cosmos and reduce it to nothing? Or does the fire refine and purify the cosmos? These questions hinge on the text's purpose, its vocabulary, and the function of "fire" in biblical theology (particularly Petrine theology).

Second Peter 3 responds to scoffers who believe the cosmos has always been the way it is and will continue as is without interruption. The Noahic flood demonstrates this is false, and it prefigures the final transition from the present creation to the emergence of new creation. Second Peter's interest is the transformation of the cosmos rather than its annihilation. The "destruction" of the Noahic world provides a pattern for the destruction of the present world, except this time it is by fire rather than water. Destruction does not involve reducing the cosmos to nothing. On the contrary, the old world is destroyed in order to inaugurate a new one.

The vocabulary does not necessarily entail annihilation. *Loosing* (translated "dissolve") is a metaphor for destruction, and the nature of the destruction is determined by context, which is given in the pattern of the Noahic "destruction" of the world. Further, *melting* (parallel with *loosing*) is apocalyptic language, common in such literature, to describe catastrophic events. It does not necessarily entail annihilation if the meaning of "elements" is heavenly bodies (such as Sun, moon, or stars), which is evident from its use in the Hebrew prophets (Isa. 24:23 [LXX]; 34:4; 63:19–64:1 [LXX]; Mic. 1:4; Hab. 3:6 [LXX]; Zech. 14:12 [LXX]). However, "elements" may refer to the removal of hostile demonic powers.[1] Whatever the case, God is cleaning up the heavens and its "elements."

Second Peter 3:10 may contain the most significant line. Everything on the earth will be "laid bare," "disclosed," or "found" (*heurethesetai*). While some translations read "burned up," critical editions of the Greek text no longer accept this reading for good reasons.[2] Also, the addition of the negative ("not found"), favored by some textual critics, lacks support from any Greek manuscripts, and it cannot explain the origin of the more difficult reading ("found" rather than "not found").

However, *heurethesetai* is a difficult reading, which is one reason it is the best reading in the light of text-critical principles. But there are reasonable options. The text may echo 1 Peter 1:7, where the "genuineness" of faith is "found" (*heurethe*) through suffering "trials" (*peirasmois*). The judgment of the world, including a "fiery trial" (1 Peter 4:12; cf. 4:16–17), involves finding or laying bare the earth and its works through fire.

This fire, like elsewhere in Petrine theology (1 Peter 1:7; 4:12), is a refining, discerning, and purifying one. Malachi 3:1–4 may lie in the background—an early Christian thought so in 2 Clement 16:3. The fire destroys what is corrupt but preserves what is authentic. It is a smelting process out of which something pure, new, and authentic emerges. It is like burning a field in order to clear the ground for a new crop. A "new heaven and new earth" will arise from the old one.

What, then, is the nature of this "new heaven and new earth"? It has both continuity and discontinuity with the present heaven and earth. The present cosmos is refined by fire and thus the "old" world is destroyed. But the "new" world is a material reality—it is a "new *earth*." Just as the Noahic world was destroyed but continued in a new way, so this present cosmos will be destroyed and continue in a new way.

"Heavens and earth" describes the reality of the cosmos in the three habitable worlds. Just as the first world God created was material and physical, and just as the present world is material and physical, so the future new heaven and new earth is also material and physical. There is no reason to suppose the "new heaven and earth" is any less material than the others. It is "new" (and thus different—a transformed or transfigured reality) but it is still the "heavens and the earth."

1 Thessalonians 4:16–17

> For the Lord himself, with a cry of command, with the
> archangel's call and with the sound of God's trumpet, will
> descend from heaven, and the dead in Christ will rise first.
> Then we who are alive, who are left, will be caught up in the
> clouds together with them to meet the Lord in the air; and so
> we will be with the Lord forever.

Roman colonists settled Thessalonica during the first decades of
the imperial period, which enhanced the imperial cult (religion)
within the city. The city even minted coins identifying Caesar as
theos (god). First Thessalonians is filled with allusions to this imperial hegemony, including (1) "peace and security" (1 Thess. 5:3),
which is what the empire claimed; (2) Jesus as "Lord" (1 Thess. 1:3,
6, 8; 2:15, 19; 3:8, 11–13; 4:1–2, 6, 15–17; 5:2, 9, 12, 23) when the empire
claimed Caesar is Lord; and (3) *parousia* (coming; 1 Thess. 2:19; 3:13;
4:15; 5:23), which is the arrival of a imperial dignitary. In fact, the
"coming of the Lord," which only appears in 1 Thessalonians (3:13;
4:15; 5:23), expects the arrival of the King of Kings.

Imperial language saturates 1 Thessalonians 4:13–18. Recognizing this illuminates a key term in the text. We will "meet"
(*apantesin*) the Lord in the air. It is a technical word for the formal
reception of a dignitary. The term describes how city officials and
leading citizens would go outside the city walls to meet dignitaries
and then escort them back into the city. This specific use of *apantesin* is widespread in the Greco-Roman world,[3] and it appears with
this meaning in Acts 28:15 when Jewish leaders met Paul outside
Rome and escorted him into the city. The only other use of the
term in the New Testament is Matthew 25:6 when the virgins come
out to meet the bridegroom and escort him back into the banquet.

Paul describes this scenario:

1. The Lord comes (*parousia*), which is the return of the king.
2. The Lord descends from heaven, where he presently reigns.
3. The dead in Christ rise first.
4. Those who are yet alive "meet" the returning king in the air and return with the king to the earth.
5. The saints will then forever be with the Lord.

Paul does not say we will be with the Lord in the air forever. Rather, we will "meet" the Lord in the air and then escort him back to the earth like a returning, triumphant king. And there—upon the earth—we will forever be with the Lord.

This is no "rapture" into the heavens where we will live forever. On the contrary, we go out to "meet" the returning King, and then we will live and reign with him forever upon God's new earth. This is no millennial reign, which lasts for only a thousand years. It is an eternal one.

Given the meaning of 2 Peter 3, we might imagine the following scenario: Jesus returns to gather his people from the earth (the dead and the living) so that we "meet him in the air." The earth is destroyed, purified, and renewed by fire while we are "in the air" with Jesus. When the destruction is past and the new earth emerges, we return with the king to the new earth where the kingdom of God will fill the whole earth.

That is our Christian hope—raised from the dead, we will reign with the King of Glory forever upon God's good but new earth.

Historic Stone-Campbell Perspectives

Though both the "spiritual vision model" and the "new creation model" are present in historic Christianity, "transformation, not annihilation," writes Althaus, is the widely "held doctrine from Irenaeus onwards, by way of Augustine and Gregory the Great, Aquinas and the whole of medieval theology, down to present-day Catholic dogmatics."[4] It was also the view of Martin Luther and John Calvin as well as Calvin's heirs in the Reformed Tradition.[5]

Many nineteenth-century Stone-Campbell (or American Restoration) Movement leaders believed future redemption included the regeneration of the spirit, body, and cosmos. God will refine the cosmos by fire and transform it into a new heaven and new earth, just as God will raise our bodies from the grave and transform them into bodies animated by the Holy Spirit fitted for living on the new earth.

Alexander Campbell and Walter Scott

For Campbell, there are two modes of regeneration, "moral and physical."[6] The former is the "renovation of the mind," while the latter is the "renovation of the body." He first describes moral regeneration, then he describes "physical regeneration," which is the *"immortality of the body."* Campbell explicitly rejects "the doctrine of Plato." As the "Head of the New Creation," the resurrected body of Jesus is the pattern for our own—"this is the Christian hope."

Physical regeneration is cosmic, including the "new creation of the heavens and the earth." While the "present elements" will be "changed by fire," this does not annihilate the material universe. "God re-creates, regenerates, but annihilates nothing." The earth, like our bodies, is redeemed and primed for eternal existence. Indeed, the "resurrection of the body, its transformation and that of the earth, are almost coincident events."[7] Just as our resurrected bodies are material regenerations of our present bodies, so the renewed material universe is a "second edition of the heavens and earth."[8] Humanity will live with God on the "new earth, the everlasting home of man; for the tabernacle of God is to be there forever."[9]

Scott saw God's redemptive scheme play out in three successive worlds: the worlds of Adam, Noah, and Abraham. "The Bible," he writes, speaks of "one globe [formed] into three habitable worlds"— the "primitive," "present," and "future." These correspond to the worlds Adam inhabited (primitive), Noah inaugurated (present), and Abraham was promised (future).

Just as the present world was "formed out of the ruins of the first and original one, so the third and future world shall, by the power of God, be constructed from the ashes of the present one." The "present habitable globe," like the primitive one, will be destroyed, but "from the ashes will rise another heaven and another earth . . . the abode of [the] righteous." This is "the new heavens and new earth . . . created at the second coming of our Lord Jesus Christ." This "new earth" is the inheritance promised Abraham (Rom. 4:13), and it is the "hope of all Christians."[10]

The Nashville Bible School

Though many associate a renewed earth with fringe groups (e.g., Jehovah's Witnesses), it was common among Churches of Christ in the late nineteenth century, especially David Lipscomb and James A. Harding, cofounders of the Nashville Bible School (now Lipscomb University).

What exactly did they mean, and why was it important to them?

Creation. When God created the cosmos, God came to dwell with humanity. The Garden of Eden was God's sanctuary, and God communed with humanity. God shared dominion with humanity and equipped them as vice regents on the earth.

Fall. However, humanity turned the cosmos "over to Satan," and a war began between the kingdom of God and the "kingdoms of this world, under the leadership of Satan."[11] God, in one sense, "left this world as a dwelling place,"[12] and now Satan "dwells upon the earth" to deceive the nations and devour Christians.[13]

Messianic Age. Beginning with Israel and revealed in Jesus, God restores dominion over the cosmos through a kingdom people whose lives reflect God's glory. God drew near to Israel by dwelling in the temple, then came to dwell in the flesh, and now dwells in Christians by the Spirit. God's redemptive mission is presently advanced through the church in the power of the Spirit.

New Creation. God's mission is to fully dwell upon the earth, fill it with divine glory, and restore the reign of God in the cosmos. On that day, when the heavenly Jerusalem descends to the new earth, "God will take up his abode himself with his great family upon this new, this renovated and purified earth."[14] Then the meek will inherit the earth (Matt. 5:5), and all children of Abraham—through faith in the Messiah—will inherit the cosmos (Rom. 4:13).

Creation—both humanity and the cosmos—is lost, then contested, and ultimately won and purified. On that day, Lipscomb writes, "*earth itself shall become heaven*."[15] God's good creation, then, is regained and renewed rather than annihilated or eternally lost. Creation again becomes God's home.

Selected Creation

New Creation Texts in Scripture

Torah

Genesis 1–3: Creation and Vandalism

Genesis 9:8–17: God's Covenant with Creation

Exodus 14: Creation in the Service of Salvation

Exodus 23:12 (Deut. 5:14): Sabbath Rest for Animals

Leviticus 25: Jubilee for Creation

Deuteronomy 15: Creation, Sabbath, and the Poor

Psalms

Psalm 8: Creation and Human Vocation

Psalm 19: Creation, Torah, and God's Glory

Psalm 33: Creation as Act of Justice

Psalm 65: God Clothes Creation

Psalm 96: Inviting Creation to Praise God

Psalm 104: Creation as God's Art

Psalm 136: The Steadfast Love of the Lord Endures Forever

Psalm 148: Creation's Worship of the Creator

Wisdom

Job 12:7–10: The Wisdom of Animals

Job 26:7–14: God's Work within Creation

Job 38–41: God's Intimate Relation with Creation

Proverbs 6: 6–11: God's Wisdom in the Ant

Proverbs 8: Creation and Wisdom

Proverbs 30:18–19: Creation and Wonder

Ecclesiastes 3:1–15: God's Work within Creation

Ecclesiastes 9:7–10: Delighting in Creation

Ecclesiastes 12:1–7: Remember Your Creator

The Prophets

Isaiah 9:1–7: The Restoration of God's Kingdom in the Land

Isaiah 11:1–10: The Restoration of God's Kingdom in the Land

Isaiah 24:4–13: Groaning of Creation

Isaiah 25: Banquet on the New Earth

Isaiah 32: Creation, Justice, and Salvation

Isaiah 35: Creation's Renewal

Isaiah 43:13–21: Salvation and Creation

Isaiah 65–66: The Promise of New Heavens and New Earth

Ezekiel 34:17–18: Human Abuse of Creation

Hosea 3:16–23: Covenant with the Animals for Israel

Hosea 4:1–3: Creation Suffers due to Human Sin

Joel 2: Resurrection of the Land and the Pouring Out of God's Spirit ·

Habakkuk 2:17: Woe upon Human Violence to the Earth

Zechariah 14: When God Will Reign over All the Earth

Gospels and Acts

Luke 4:16–21: The Jubilee Ministry of Jesus

Luke 24:36–49: The Resurrection of the Material Body of Jesus

John 1:1–5, 14–18: The Word Completes Creation through Incarnation

John 20:24–29: Jesus, Thomas, and the Resurrection

Acts 14:15–18: Creation Bears Witness to God

Acts 17:22–31: God's Presence within Creation

Epistles

Romans 1:18–21: Creation Testifies to God

Romans 8: The Redemption of Creation

1 Corinthians 15: The Promise of Resurrection

Colossians 1:15–20: Jesus, Creator and Redeemer of All Things

Hebrews 1:1–4: The Son as Sustainer and Heir of Creation

2 Peter 3:1–13: Purification of Creation

Revelation

Revelation 4–5: The Praise of All Creation and the Reign of Humanity with Jesus

Revelation 11:15–18: The Kingdom of this World Becomes the Kingdom of God

Revelation 21–22: God Dwells within the New Creation with Humanity

Suggested Resources

Biblical Theology

Beale, Gregory K. *The Temple and the Church's Mission: A Biblical Theology of the Dwelling Place of God.* Downers Grove, IL: InterVarsity Press, 2004.

Block, Daniel, and Noah J. Toy, eds. *Keeping God's Earth: The Global Environment in Biblical Perspective.* Downers Grove, IL: InterVarsity Press, 2010.

Middleton, J. Richard. *A New Heaven and a New Earth: Reclaiming Biblical Eschatology.* Grand Rapids, MI: Baker, 2014.

Moo, Jonathan, and Robert S. White. *Let Creation Rejoice: Biblical Hope and Ecological Crisis.* Downers Grove, IL: InterVarsity Press, 2014.

Pennington, Jonathan T., and Sean M. McDoough, eds. *Cosmology and New Testament Theology.* Edinburgh: T. & T. Clark, 2008.

Walton, John H. *The Lost World of Genesis One.* Downers Grove, IL: InterVarsity Press, 2009.

Wolters, Albert M. *Creation Regained.* Grand Rapids, MI: Eerdmans, 1985.

Wright, Christopher. *The Mission of God's People: A Biblical Theology of the Church's Mission.* Grand Rapids, MI: Zondervan, 2010.

Wright, N. T. *Surprised by Hope: Rethinking Heaven, the Resurrection, and the Mission of the Church.* San Francisco: HarperOne, 2007.

Contemporary Environmental Ethics

Berry, R. J., ed. *The Care of Creation: Focusing Concern and Action.* Downers Grove, IL: InterVarsity Press, 2000.

Louv, Richard. *Last Child in the Woods: Saving Our Children from Nature-Deficit Disorder.* Chapel Hill, NC: Algonquin Books of Chapel Hill, 2005.

Robinson, Tri, and Jason Chatraw. *Saving God's Green Earth: Rediscovering the Church's Responsibility to Environmental Stewardship.* Norcross, GA: Ampelon Publishing, 2006.

Van Dyke, Fred, David C. Mahan, Joseph K. Sheldon, and Raymond H. Brand. *Redeeming Creation: The Biblical Basis for Environmental Stewardship.* Downers Grove, IL: InterVarsity Press, 1996.

Wilson, E. O. *The Creation: An Appeal to Save Life on Earth.* New York: W. W. Norton, 2006.

Practicing Resurrection in Community

James, Larry. *The Wealth of the Poor: How Valuing Every Neighbor Restores Hope in Our Cities.* Abilene, TX: Abilene Christian University Press, 2013.

Harris, Maria. *Proclaim Jubilee!: A Spirituality for the Twenty-First Century.* Louisville: Westminster John Knox, 1996.

McKnight, Scott. *The Jesus Creed: Loving God, Loving Others.* Brewster, MA: Paraclete Press, 2004.

Pohl, Christine D. *Making Room: Recovering Hospitality as a Christian Tradition.* Grand Rapids, MI: Eerdmans, 1999.

Science and Creation

Harris, Mark. *The Nature of Creation: Examining the Bible and Science.* New York: Routledge, 2014.

Polkinghorne, John. *The God of Hope and the End of the World.* New Haven: Yale University Press, 2003.

Wilkinson, David. *The Christian Eschatology and the Physical Universe.* Edinburgh: T. & T. Clark, 2010.

Thinking about Heaven

Alcorn, Randy. *Heaven.* Carol Stream, IL: Tyndale House Publishers, 2004.

Kreeft, Peter. *Everything You Ever Wanted to Know about Heaven but Never Dreamed of Asking.* San Francisco: Ignatius Press, 1990.

McKnight, Scott. *The Heaven Promise: Engaging the Bibles Truth about Life to Come.* Colorado Springs: WaterBrook Press, 2015.

Digging Deeper

Braaten, Laurie. "Earth Community in Joel 1–2: A Call to Identify with the Rest of Creation." *Horizons in Biblical Theology* 28, no. 2 (2006): 113–29.

———. "The Groaning of Creation: The Biblical Background for Romans 8:22." *Biblical Research* 50 (2005): 19–39.

Bruno, Christopher. "Jesus Is Our Jubilee . . . But How? The OT Background and Lukan Fulfillment of the Ethics of Jubilee." *Journal of the Evangelical Theological Society* 53 (2010): 81–101.

Chryssavgis, John. "A New Heaven and New Earth: Orthodox Theology and an Ecological World View." *Ecumenical Review* 62, no. 2 (July 2010): 214–22.

Greenspoon, Leonard. "From Dominion to Stewardship? The Ecology of Biblical Translation." In *Religion and the Environment*, edited by Ronald A. Simkins. *Journal of Religion and Society Supplement* Series 3 (2008). Accessed September 1, 2015. http://moses.creighton.edu/JRS/toc/SS03.html.

Heide, Gale. "What Is New about the New Heaven and New Earth?" *Journal for the Evangelical Theological Society* 40, no. 1 (March 1997): 37–56.

Jeremias, Joachim. "Flesh and Blood Cannot Inherit the Kingdom of God." *New Testament Studies* 2, no. 3 (1956): 151–59.

Kawashima, Robert S. "The Jubilee Year and the Return of Cosmic Purity." *Catholic Biblical Quarterly* 65, no. 3 (2003): 370–89.

LeMasters, Philip. "Incarnation, Sacrament, and the Environment in Orthodox Thought." *Worship* 81, no. 3 (May 2007): 212–26.

Moo, Douglas. "Nature in New Creation." *Journal for the Evangelical Theological Society* 49, no. 3 (2006): 449–88.

Ruston, Kathleen P. "The Cosmology of John 1:1–14 and Its Implications for Ethical Action in This Ecological Age." *Colloquium* 45, no. 2 (2013): 127–53.

Ryan, Juza. "Echoes of Sodom and Gomorrah on the Davy of the Lord: Intertextuality and Tradition in 2 Peter 3:7–13." *Bulletin for Biblical Research* 24 (2014): 227–45.

VanGemeren, Williem A. "The Spirit of Restoration." *Westminster Theological Journal* 50, no. 1 (1988): 81–102.

Van Leeuwen, Raymond C. "Cosmos, Temple, House: Building and Wisdom in Mesopotamia and Israel." In *Wisdom Literature in Mesopotamia and Israel*, edited by Richard C. Cliff, 67–90. Atlanta: Society of Biblical Literature in Mesopotamia, 2007.

Wolters, Albert M. "Worldview and Textual Criticism in 2 Peter 3:10." *Westminster Theological Journal* 49, no. 2 (1987): 405–13.

Websites for Calculating Environmental and Carbon Footprints

http://footprint.wwf.org.uk

http://www.nature.org/greenliving/carboncalculator

http://www.terrapass.com/carbon-footprint-calculator

http://www3.epa.gov/carbon-footprint-calculator

Notes

Introduction

[1] N. T. Wright, *Simply Christian* (London: Society for Promoting Christian Knowledge, 2006), 186.

Chapter One

[1] Ira Stanphill, "Mansion over the Hilltop," 1949.

[2] Albert E. Brumley, "This World Is Not My Home," 1937.

[3] James W. Acuff, "Just over in the Glory Land," 1906.

[4] James M. Black, "When the Roll Is Called up Yonder," 1893.

[5] Charles Wesley, "Love Divine, All Love Excelling," 1747.

[6] "Jehovah Will Rejoice in His Works," *Hymns of Hope*, ed. William Norton (London: E. Stock Company, 1879), 747.

[7] "Dark Places Full of Cruelty," *Hymns*, 515.

[8] Craig A. Blaising, "Premillennialism," in *Three Views on the Millennium and Beyond*, ed. Darrell L. Bock (Grand Rapids, MI: Zondervan, 1999), 161–62.

[9] Collen McDannel and Bernhard Lang, *Heaven: A History* (New Haven: Yale University Press, 1988), 57, citing *Poimandres* from the *Corpus Hermeticum*.

[10] Irenaeus, *Treatise on Resurrection*, 44.

[11] Irenaeus, *Against Heresies* 2.10.4.

[12] *Against Heresies*, 4.6.7.

[13] *Against Heresies*, 3.18.1.

[14] *Against Heresies* 5.36.1.

[15] *Against Heresies*, 5.36.3.

[16] *MacArthur Study Bible* (Nashville: Thomas Nelson, 2013), c.v. 2 Peter 3:7–12.

Chapter Two

[1] Ellen Davis, *Getting Involved with God: Rediscovering the Old Testament* (Cambridge: Cowley, 2001), 192–94.

Chapter Three

[1] *Familiar Lectures on the Pentateuch* (repr.; Rosemead, CA: Old Paths Book Club, 1958), 273.

[2] Terence E. Fretheim, "Nature's Praise of God in the Psalms," *Ex Auditu* 3 (1987): 22.

Chapter Four

[1] See the parallel between the Leviathan and the "Sea" in Job 3:8.

Chapter Five

[1] *Salvation from Sin* (Nashville: McQuiddy, 1913), 11.

Chapter Six

[1] "Regeneration," *Millennial Harbinger Extra* 4 (August 1833), 358–59.

Chapter Seven

[1] Quoted in Maria Harris, *Proclaim Jubilee!: A Spirituality for the Twenty-First Century* (Louisville: Westminster John Knox, 1996), 94.

[2] The Melchizedek Text (11QMelch), as cited by James C. Vanderkam, *The Dead Sea Scrolls Today*, 2nd ed. (Grand Rapids, MI: Eerdmans, 2010), 73–74.

Chapter Eight

[1] "Three Lessons from the Book of Romans," in *Biographies and Sermons*, ed. F. D. Srygley (Nashville: McQuiddy, 1898), 249.

Chapter Nine

[1] Jonathan Moo, "The Sea That Is No More: Revelation 21.1 and the Function of Sea Imagery in the Apocalypse of John," *Novum Testamentum* 51 (2009): 148–67.

Chapter Ten

[1] Eugene Peterson, *Practice Resurrection: A Conversation on Growing up in Christ* (Grand Rapids, MI: Eerdmans, 2010), 12.

Chapter Eleven

[1] Steven R. Harmon and Paul Avis, *Towards Baptist Catholicity: Essays on Tradition and Baptist Vision* (Eugene, OR: Wipf and Stock, 2006), 163.

[2]John Mark Hicks, *Enter the Water, Come to the Table: Baptism and the Lord's Supper in God's Story of New Creation* (Abilene, TX: Abilene Christian University Press, 2014); and John Mark Hicks, Johnny Melton, and Bobby Valentine, *A Gathered People* (Abilene, TX: Leafwood Publishers, 2007). Material in this chapter previously appeared in *Enter the Water, Come to the Table*.

Chapter Twelve

[1]Aldo Leopold and Charles Walsh Schwartz, "The Land Ethic," in *A Sand County Almanac: With Other Essays on Conservation from Round River* (New York: Oxford University Press, 1966), 239.

[2]Lynn White, "The Historic Roots of our Ecological Crisis," *Science* 155 (1967): 1206.

[3]Jimmy Carter, *Our Endangered Values: America's Moral Crisis* (New York: Simon & Schuster, 2005), 19.

[4]Leopold and Schwartz, "Land Ethic," 246, emphasis ours.

[5]Heather H. Boyd, "Christianity and the Environment in the American Public," *Journal for the Scientific Study of Religion* 38, no. 1 (March 1999): 36.

[6]Ibid., 42; Douglas L. Eckberg and T. Jean Blocker, "Christianity, Environmentalism, and the Theoretical Problem of Fundamentalism," *Journal for the Scientific Study of Religion* 35, no. 4 (December 1996): 343.

[7]R. B. Fowler, *The Greening of Protestant Thought* (Chapel Hill: University of North Carolina Press, 1995), 46–47.

[8]Pew Research Center: Religion and Public Life, "Few Say Religion Shapes Immigration, Environment Views," accessed September 10, 2015, http://www.pewforum.org/2010/09/17/few-say-religion-shapes-immigration-environment-views.

[9]Sustainable Sanctuary Coalition, "Interview with Rev. Richard Cizik," accessed September 9, 2013, http://ssckc.org/wp-content/uploads/2012/06/The-Great-Warming-Interview-with-Rev-Cizik.pdf, emphasis ours.

[10]Hal Lindsey, *The Late Great Planet Earth* (Grand Rapids, MI: Zondervan, 1970).

[11]Tim Lahaye and Jerry B. Jenkins, *Left Behind: A Novel of the Earth's Last Days* (Carol Stream, IL: Tyndale House Publishers, 1995).

[12]Al Truesdale, "Last Things First: The Impact of Eschatology on Ecology," *Perspectives on Science and Christian Faith* 46, no. 2 (June 1994): 116.

Chapter Thirteen

[1]Aldo Leopold and Charles Walsh Schwartz, "The Land Ethic," in *A Sand County Almanac: With Other Essays on Conservation from Round River* (New York: Oxford University Press, 1966), 262.

[2] Pope Francis, *Ludato Si'* [Encyclical Letter on Care for Our Common Home], Chapter 1: sec. 42, accessed September 11, 2015, http://w2.vatican.va /content/francesco/en/encyclicals/documents/papa-francesco_20150524 _enciclica-laudato-si.html.

[3] Seafood Watch, "Wild Seafood," Monterey Bay Aquarium, accessed September 8, 2015, http://www.seafoodwatch.org/ocean-issues/wild-seafood.

[4] National Oceanic and Atmospheric Administration, "Choosing Sustainable," *Fish Watch*, accessed September 8, 2015, http://www.fishwatch .gov/buying_seafood/choosing_sustainable.htm.

[5] http://www.seafoodwatch.org.

[6] US Committee of the North American Bird Conservation Initiative, "State of the Birds 2014," accessed September 8, 2015, http://www.stateofthebirds.org /newsroom/2014_State_of_the_Birds_Release.pdf.

[7] US Fish and Wildlife Service, "Duck Stamp: Put Your Stamp on Conservation," accessed September 13, 2015, http://www.fws.gov/birds/get -involved/duck-stamp.php.

[8] Humane Farm Animal Care, "Our Mission," accessed September 8, 2015, http://certifiedhumane.org.

[9] US Fish and Wildlife Service, "National Wildlife Refuge System," accessed September 8, 2015, http://www.fws.gov/refuges.

[10] Monarch Watch, University of Kansas, accessed September 8, 2015, http:// www.monarchwatch.org.

[11] Smithsonian Migratory Bird Center, "Bird Friendly Coffee," Smithsonian National Zoological Park Conservation Biology Institute, accessed September 13, 2015, http://nationalzoo.si.edu/scbi/migratorybirds/coffee.

Chapter Fourteen

[1] Alexander Campbell, "Replication, No. II. to Spencer Clack," *Christian Baptist* 5 (September 3, 1827), in *Christian Baptist, Seven Volumes in One*, ed. D. S. Burnet (Joplin, MO: College Press, 1983), 369–70.

[2] Thomas H. Olbricht, "Recovery of Covenantal Narratival Biblical Theology in the Restoration Movement," in *And the Word Became Flesh: Studies in History, Communication, and Scripture in Memory of Michael W. Casey*, ed. Thomas H. Olbricht and David Fleer (Eugene, OR: Pickwick, 2009), 72–88.

[3] Alexander Campbell, "The Gospel," *Millennial Harbinger* 36, no. 11 (November 1865): 517.

[4] Alexander Campbell, "Grace, Faith, Repentance, Baptism, Regeneration, No. 1," *Millennial Harbinger* 5th Series, 2, no. 3 (March 1859): 130.

Appendix

[1] Ryan Juza, "Echoes of Sodom and Gomorrah on the Day of the Lord: Intertextuality and Tradition in 2 Peter 3:7–13," *Bulletin for Biblical Research* 24 (2014): 227–45.

[2] A convenient place to see the evidence is Daniel Wallace, "A Brief Note on a Textual Problem in 2 Peter 3:10," accessed November 23, 2015, https://bible.org/article/brief-note-textual-problem-2-peter-310.

[3] See the numerous citations Bobby Valentine supplies at http://stonedcampbelldisciple.com/2011/03/10/paul-the-roman-imperial-cult-the-return-of-king-jesus-and-flying-away-in-1-thessalonians-4-17.

[4] As quoted by Jurgen Moltmann, *The Coming of God: Christian Eschatology* (Minneapolis: Fortress Press, 1996), 268.

[5] Francis Turretin, *Institutes of Elenctic Theology*, ed. James T. Dennison Jr. and trans. George Musgrave (Phillipsburg, NJ: Presbyterian and Reformed, 1997), 3:590–91; John Gill, *Body of Divinity*, book 7, chapters 6–7, http://pbministries.org/books/gill/gills_archive.htm#2; and Charles Hodge, *Systematic Theology* (repr.; Grand Rapids, MI: Eerdmans, 1977), 3:853–54.

[6] Alexander Campbell, *Christian System* (Pittsburg, PA: Forrester & Campbell, 1839), 220, 235–37, 257.

[7] Campbell, "The Coming of the Lord—No. IV," *Millennial Harbinger* 2nd Series, 5 (March 1841): 102.

[8] Campbell, "Prophecy—No. 3," *Millennial Harbinger* 5th Series, 3 (December 1860): 668.

[9] Campbell, "The Coming of the Lord—No. II," *Millennial Harbinger* 2nd Series, 5 (February 1841): 54.

[10] Walter Scott, "Of a Succession of Worlds, and of the Great Physical Destinies of Our Globe, as Spoken of in the Scriptures," *The Evangelist* 6 (January 1838): 3–5, (February 1838): 34–35, and (April 1838): 77.

[11] James A. Harding, "For What Are We Here?" *The Way* 5 (December 1903): 1041.

[12] David Lipscomb, *Salvation from Sin* (Nashville: McQuiddy, 1913), 36.

[13] James A. Harding, "Scraps," *The Way* 4 (May 1902): 58.

[14] Harding, "For What Are We Here," 1042.

[15] Lipscomb, "The Kingdom of God," *Gospel Advocate* 45 (May 1903): 328, emphasis ours.

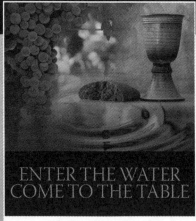
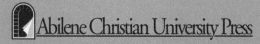

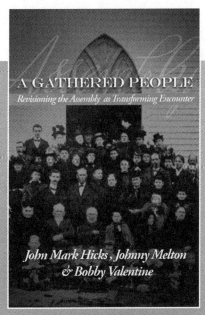